While the work of Henri Lefebvre has become better known in the English-speaking world since the 1991 translation of his 1974 masterpiece, *The Production of Space*, his influence on the actual production of architecture and the city has been less pronounced. Although now widely read in schools of architecture, planning and urban design, Lefebvre's message for practice remains elusive, inevitably so because the entry of his work into the Anglosphere has come with repression of the two most challenging aspects of his thinking: Romanticism and Utopia, which simultaneously confront modernity while being progressive.

Contemporary discomfort with Romanticism and Utopia arguably obstructs the shift of Lefebvre's thinking from being objects of theoretical interest into positions of actually influencing practices. Attempting to understand and act upon architecture and the city with Lefebvre but without Utopia and Romanticism risks muting the impact of his ideas. Although Utopia may seem to have no place in the present, Lefebvre reveals this as little more than a self-serving affirmation that 'there is no alternative' to social and political detachment. Demanding the impossible may end in failure but as Lefebvre shows us, doing so is the first step towards other possibilities. To think with Lefebvre is to think about Utopia; doing so makes contact with what is most enduring about his project for the city and its inhabitants, and with what is most radical about it as well.

Lefebvre for Architects offers a concise account of the relevance of Henri Lefebvre's writing for the theory and practice of architecture, planning and urban design. This book is accessible for students and practitioners who wish to fully engage with the design possibilities offered by Lefebvre's philosophy.

Nathaniel Coleman is Reader in History and Theory of Architecture at Newcastle University, UK. He previously taught in the US, and practiced architecture in New York, USA, and Rome, Italy. Author of *Utopias and Architecture* (2005) and editor of *Imagining and Making the World: Reconsidering architecture and Utopia* (2011), Nathaniel recently guest-edited a special issue on architecture of the journal *Utopian Studies* (2014). He has published numerous journal articles and book chapters, and presented his research on the problem of architecture and Utopia internationally. He is particularly interested in the convergences of architectural history, theory and design with Utopia's generative potential.

Thinkers for Architects

Series Editor: Adam Sharr, Newcastle University, UK

Editorial Board

Jonathan A. Hale, University of Nottingham, UK
Hilde Heynen, KU Leuven, Netherlands
David Leatherbarrow, University of Pennsylvania, USA

Architects have often looked to philosophers and theorists from beyond the discipline for design inspiration or in search of a critical framework for practice. This original series offers quick, clear introductions to key thinkers who have written about architecture and whose work can yield insights for designers.

> 'Each unintimidatingly slim book makes sense of the subjects' complex theories.'
>
> **Building Design**

> '. . . a valuable addition to any studio space or computer lab.'
>
> **Architectural Record**

> '. . . a creditable attempt to present their subjects in a useful way.'
>
> **Architectural Review**

Deleuze and Guattari for Architects
Andrew Ballantyne

Heidegger for Architects
Adam Sharr

Irigaray for Architects
Peg Rawes

Bhabha for Architects
Felipe Hernández

Bourdieu for Architects
Helena Webster

Benjamin for Architects
Brian Elliott

Derrida for Architects
Richard Coyne

Gadamer for Architects
Paul Kidder

Foucault for Architects
Gordana Fontana-Giusti

Goodman for Architects
Remei Capdevila-Werning

Lefebvre for Architects
Nathaniel Coleman

Virilio for Architects
John Armitage

Baudrillard for Architects
Francesco Proto

Kant for Architects
Diane Morgan

Merleau-Ponty for Architects
Jonathan Hale

THINKERS FOR ARCHITECTS

Lefebvre
for
Architects

Nathaniel Coleman

LONDON AND NEW YORK

First published 2015
by Routledge
2 Park Square, Milton Park, Abingdon, Oxon OX14 4RN

and by Routledge
711 Third Avenue, New York, NY 10017

Routledge is an imprint of the Taylor & Francis Group, an informa business.

© 2015 Nathaniel Coleman

The right of Nathaniel Coleman to be identified as author of this work has been asserted by him in accordance with sections 77 and 78 of the Copyright, Designs and Patents Act 1988.

All rights reserved. No part of this book may be reprinted or reproduced or utilised in any form or by any electronic, mechanical or other means, now known or hereafter invented, including photocopying and recording, or in any information storage or retrieval system, without permission in writing from the publishers.

Trademark notice: Product or corporate names may be trademarks or registered trademarks, and are used only for identification and explanation without intent to infringe.

British Library Cataloguing-in-Publication Data
A catalogue record for this book is available from the British Library.

Library of Congress Cataloging-in-Publication Data
Coleman, Nathaniel, 1961–
  Lefebvre for architects / Nathaniel Coleman.
    pages cm. — (Thinkers for architects)
  Includes bibliographical references and index.
  1. Lefebvre, Henri, 1901–1991. 2. Architecture and philosophy. 3. Visionary architecture. 4. Utopias. 5. Architecture—Philosophy. 6. Architecture and society. I. Title.
  NA2500.C57 2015
  720.1—dc23
  2014025868

ISBN: 978-0-415-63939-2 (hbk)
ISBN: 978-0-415-63940-8 (pbk)
ISBN: 978-1-315-73654-9 (ebk)

Typeset in Frutiger and Galliard
by Apex CoVantage, LLC

Printed and bound in Great Britain by
TJ International Ltd, Padstow, Cornwall

To P, Z and E

'Change life!' 'Change society!' These precepts mean nothing without the production of an appropriate space. [. . .] To change life, [. . .] we must first change space.

Lefebvre, *Production of Space*, pp. 59, 190

The architect occupies an especially uncomfortable position. As a scientist and technician, obliged to produce within a specified framework, he has to depend on repetition. In his search for inspiration as an artist, and as someone sensitive to use and to the 'user', however, he has a stake in difference. He is located willy-nilly within this painful contradiction, forever being shuttled from one of its poles to the other. His is the difficult task of bridging the gap between product and work, and he is fated to live out the conflicts that arise as he desperately seeks to close the ever-widening gulf between knowledge and creativity.

Lefebvre, *Production of Space*, p. 396

Surely there comes a moment when formalism is exhausted, when only a new injection of content into form can destroy it and so open up the way to innovation.

Lefebvre, *Production of Space*, p. 145

No sooner is Marx pronounced dead than Marxism experiences a resurgence. [. . .] The scientific and technological changes of the modern world have now made a reconsideration of Marxist thought inevitable. The thesis presented here might be summarized as follows. Each of the concepts of Marxism may be taken up once more, and carried to a higher level, without any significant moment of the theory as a whole being lost. On the other hand, if they are considered in the setting of Marx's exposition, these concepts and their theoretical articulation no longer have an object. The renewal of Marx's concepts is best effected by taking full account of space.

Lefebvre, *Production of Space*, pp. 342–343

Contents

Series editor's preface	xiii
Illustration credits	xv
Acknowledgements	xvii

1. Introduction: Lefebvre for architects   1

Lefebvre for architects 1
The problematic of architecture 4
Lefebvre and architecture 11
Architecture thinking its own thoughts 15

2. Utopia and a new Romanticism   18

Utopia as the prospect of the possible 18
Romanticism and Utopia 20
Generate and degenerate Utopias 25
Critiques of everyday life 33
There is no alternative? Or, Lefebvre and Utopia 34
Lefebvre's other vision of Utopia 38
Dialectical utopianism 42
Experimental and theoretical Utopias 44
The Utopian prospect of Lefebvre 51

3. The production of space   53

Problematic of *The Production of Space* 53
From space to place 56
Overcoming Cartesian logic 59
Representations of the relations of production 62

Recuperating the social 63

Repetition everywhere 69

Spatial codes 72

Spatial practice/representations of space/representational space 79

The antithesis of systems 85

4. *Rhythmanalysis* and the timespace of the city   91

Rhythmanalysis and different spaces 94

Collapsing dualities 98

Elements of rhythmanalysis 101

The relativity of rhythms 104

Paris and the Mediterranean 108

The perils of capital 117

The rhythmanalyst and the architect 120

5. Conclusion: another scale?   124

Further reading   129

Bibliography   131

Index   137

Series editor's preface

Adam Sharr

Architects have often looked to thinkers in philosophy and theory for design ideas, or in search of a critical framework for practice. Yet architects and students of architecture can struggle to navigate thinkers' writings. It can be daunting to approach original texts with little appreciation of their contexts. And existing introductions seldom explore a thinker's architectural material in any detail. This original series offers clear, quick and accurate introductions to key thinkers who have written about architecture. Each book summarises what a thinker has to offer for architects. It locates their architectural thinking in the body of their work, introduces significant books and essays, helps decode terms and provides quick reference for further reading. If you find philosophical and theoretical writing about architecture difficult, or just don't know where to begin, this series will be indispensable.

Books in the *Thinkers for Architects* series come out of architecture. They pursue architectural modes of understanding, aiming to introduce a thinker to an architectural audience. Each thinker has a unique and distinctive ethos, and the structure of each book derives from the character at its focus. The thinkers explored are prodigious writers and any short introduction can only address a fraction of their work. Each author – an architect or an architectural critic – has focused on a selection of a thinker's writings which they judge most relevant to designers and interpreters of architecture. Inevitably, much will be left out. These books will be the first point of reference, rather than the last word, about a particular thinker for architects. It is hoped that they will encourage you to read further, offering an incentive to delve deeper into the original writings of a particular thinker.

The *Thinkers for Architects* series has proved highly successful, expanding now to eleven volumes dealing with familiar cultural figures whose writings have influenced architectural designers, critics and commentators in distinctive and important ways. Books explore the work of: Gilles Deleuze and Felix Guattari; Martin Heidegger; Luce Irigaray; Homi Bhabha; Pierre Bourdieu; Walter Benjamin; Jacques Derrida; Hans-Georg Gadamer; Michael Foucault; Nelson Goodman and now, importantly, Henri Lefebvre. A number of future volumes are projected, addressing the work of Paul Virilio, Jean Baudrillard and Maurice Merleau-Ponty. The series continues to expand, addressing an increasingly rich diversity of contemporary thinkers who have something to say to architects.

Adam Sharr is Professor of Architecture at the University of Newcastle upon Tyne, UK; Principal of Adam Sharr Architects; and Editor (with Richard Weston) of *arq: Architectural Research Quarterly*, a Cambridge University Press international architecture journal. His books published by Routledge include *Heidegger for Architects* and *Reading Architecture and Culture*.

Illustration credits

1. Introduction: Lefebvre for architects

    1. Photo of Lefebvre, Amsterdam, Holland, 9 March 1971. Photo by Bert Verhoeff/Anefo, Dutch National Archives, The Hague. Crop of original (p. 3)
    2. 'Counter-practices', Amsterdam Orphanage, Amstelveenseweg, Amsterdam (1955–1960), Aldo van Eyck, Architect. Photo by author (p. 8)
    3. 'Everyday Life: New York City in the 1970s'. Photo by author (p. 15)

2. Utopia and a new Romanticism

    4. 'A Sick City? London in the 1970s' (view toward Nicholas Hawksmoor's Christ Church Spitalfields, 1714–1729). Photo by author (p. 24)
    5. Florence, Italy, *Centro Storico* (2000). Activity by the Uffizi Gallery (1560–1581). Photo by author (p. 29)
    6. 'Designed to be Empty?', Waterloo Square, Newcastle upon Tyne, UK. Photo by author (p. 50)

3. The production of space

    7. 'City as Commodity: Computer Simulation of the *Future*?', computer image of building under construction, Newcastle upon Tyne, UK. Photo by author (p. 58)
    8. 'Infinitely Reproducible', Sixth Avenue, New York City. Photo by author (p. 71)
    9. 'Ancient Rome Intersects the Nineteenth-Century City', *Ponte Sisto* (1473–1479), from Trastevere across the Tiber to the *Centro Storico*, Rome, Italy. Photo by author (p. 75)
    10. 'Chthonian Feminine Principles Counterbalance the Priapic Masculine Ones', *Foro Romano*, Rome, Italy. Photo by author (p. 84)
    11. Sage Gateshead, Gateshead, UK, Foster + Partners, Architects (1997–2004). Photo by author (p. 88)

4. *Rhythmanalysis* and the timespace of the city

12. '*Counterforms* to Everyday Life', Amsterdam Orphanage, Amstelveenseweg, Amsterdam (1955–1960), Aldo van Eyck, Architect. Photo by author (p. 94)
13. *Centre Georges Pompidou*, Paris, France, Studio Piano & Rogers, Architects (1971–1977). Photo by author (p. 110)
14. Municipal Baths, Vals, Switzerland, Peter Zumthor (completed 1996). Photo by author (p. 121)

5. Conclusion: another scale?

15. 'Building Community: Human Tower' (training for the *Concurs de Castells de Tarragona*), Tarragona, Spain (July 2012). Photo by author (p. 126)

Acknowledgements

The following people in particular have extended their friendship and provided me with multiple overlapping forums in which to explore many of the ideas developed in this book (often unbeknownst to either of us at the time): Andrew Ballantyne, Kati Blom, Donald Dunham, Ufuk Ersoy, Michael Gardiner, Annette Giesecke, David Leatherbarrow, Ruth Levitas, Tom Moylan, Jonathan Powers, Joseph Rykwert, Lyman Tower Sargent, Adam Sharr, Adam Stock and Ed Wainwright. My teaching in the architecture studio, in seminars and through the presentation of one-off lectures has also offered me numerous opportunities to explore and test many of the ideas developed here with students.

I am forever indebted to my children for their patience in the face of my unsocial hours of academic work. I convince myself it is somehow worth it, in the conviction that my efforts might make some very modest contribution to maintaining a world they will want to live in, or could continue to imagine as possible.

Ultimately, my greatest debt of gratitude is to my wife, Elizabeth, for her steadfast support of my work, and unwavering confidence that it is worth doing, and, on a more practical level, for her close reading of drafts and insights regarding the development of this book.

CHAPTER 1

Introduction

Lefebvre for architects

> Inasmuch as they deal with socially 'real' space, one might suppose on first consideration that architecture and texts relating to architecture would be a better choice than literary texts proper. Unfortunately, any definition of architecture itself requires a prior analysis and exposition of the concept of space.

> (Lefebvre, 1991 [1974]: 15)

Lefebvre for architects

Although the work of Henri Lefebvre (1901–1991) is now fairly well known in the English-speaking world through translation and interpretation, especially since his 1974 masterpiece, *The Production of Space* was translated in 1991, his influence on the actual production of space, on architecture and the city, has been less pronounced. Even if now widely read in schools of architecture, planning and urban design, Lefebvre's message for practice remains elusive because the entry of his work into the consciousness of the Anglosphere has arguably come at the cost of repressing two of the most challenging and central aspects of his thinking on reform and renewal: Romanticism and Utopia, which simultaneously confront modernity while being progressive, in particular by identifying the tensions between social justice and modernity, especially in relation to work, community and space.

Paradoxically, contemporary discomfort with Romanticism and Utopia makes it difficult to transform Lefebvre's thinking from objects of theoretical interest into tactics for practice. Nowhere is this more pronounced than in those attempts to understand and transform architecture and the city that are supposedly influenced by Lefebvre but which attempt change without Utopia and Romanticism. Although Utopia and Romanticism may seem out of place in the present, Lefebvre's ideas on practice and the methods he elaborated rely on both; rejecting them does little more than affirm that 'there is no alternative' to social and political disengagement. Demanding the impossible may ultimately end in failure but doing so anyway is the first step towards other possibilities. To think about Lefebvre is to think about Utopia, and thinking about Utopia when thinking with Lefebvre is to make contact with what is most radical about his project for the city and its inhabitants.

Paradoxically, contemporary discomfort with Romanticism and Utopia makes it difficult to transform Lefebvre's thinking from objects of theoretical interest into tactics for practice.

This book offers a concise account of the relevance of Henri Lefebvre's writing for the theory and practice of architecture (and by association, planning and urban design as well), without shying away from his Utopianism and Romanticism or the centrality of Marx to his thinking. The main objective of this book is to highlight for architects and architecture students, as well as for planning and urban design students and practitioners, the substantial possibilities Lefebvre's work holds out for renewed practices even at a time of neoliberal consensus in which dwindling of the state, privatisation and free markets are imagined as ensuring freedom through economic growth.

Each of the chapters that follow considers the main themes of Lefebvre's thinking, including the *production of space, representation, architectural practices, everyday life, the city* and *rhythms* as a reunification of time (history; social processes) and space (geography; architectural settings), which Western thinking tends to separate. The value of this approach resides in illuminating what is most progressive in Lefebvre, not least by demonstrating the real continuing relevance of his ideas for the imagining and making of architecture and cities worthy of their inhabitants. In this way, the method employed throughout this book is in equal measure *hermeneutical*, engaging in a

Photo of Lefebvre, Amsterdam, Holland, 9 March 1971

critical interpretation of Lefebvre's thinking which in its aims is reconstructive; *phenomenological*, inasmuch as experience and sensual perception, which make the mind and identity, are given emphasis by asserting the value of qualitative understanding; and – perhaps surprisingly – *pragmatic*, insofar as the discoveries of individual experience inevitably occur within social spaces, suggesting that real social, political or architectural reform are matters of collective action informed by experience and observation of real conditions. The hybridised method employed here, which conjoins *hermeneutics, phenomenology* and *pragmatism*, links theory to practice, space to time and form to content, in identifying how the imagination and production of concrete alternatives are, as Lefebvre believed, hiding out in the plain sight of the everyday.

The aim of most books on Lefebvre is to explain his theories from an intellectual position – to render them comprehensible. A further aim of this book is to translate Lefebvre's ideas into potentialities for action (which I believe he would have approved of). The dual challenge of such a project is to render intelligible Lefebvre's thought for architects, while also demonstrating how it might be *enacted*, that is, to show how Lefebvre's theories can inform practices. However, the most significant challenge confronting such a project is to achieve the translation proposed without reducing Lefebvre's thought to a blunt instrument, that is to say, to show how it might influence the shaping and character of practices rather than simply becoming a mechanism for action or production.

The problematic of architecture

Attempting to understand how architecture might be renewed by way of Lefebvre is to raise a paradoxical situation. He was not an architect, but rather a sociologist, or more broadly, a philosopher. Thus, appealing to Lefebvre could be seen as just another example of exiting architecture to understand it before even attempting to do so from within. Withdrawing from architecture is acceptable only if, as some would have us believe, it is not a discipline in its own right. However, raising questions about architecture and seeking answers to those questions from within the discipline (in its own right) does offer the most promising avenue of research, for reimagining, rethinking and revaluing architecture (and the city). Nevertheless, not all of the questions one might ask in practice can be answered from within the discipline of architecture – from a consideration of its literature alone. Indeed, great benefit can be gained from enlisting the assistance of thinkers from beyond the discipline, who are unencumbered by its professional habits, and who can thus begin imagining otherwise unthinkable alternatives.

Architecture's own traditions of thought arguably have a limited capacity for responding to the problematic of the city taking shape since World War II (but with much earlier origins). As such, the predicament of architecture under late capitalism – during the second half of the twentieth century, and into the early twenty-first century as well – has exceeded the capacity of the discipline to respond from within. The quandary – so effectively outlined by German philosopher Ernst Bloch (1885–1977), Italian architectural historian Manfredo Tafuri (1935–1994) and American political theorist Fredric Jameson (b.1934), amongst others, including presciently by nineteenth-century English critic John Ruskin (1819–1900) and his near contemporary, designer and social reformer William Morris (1834–1896) before them – concerns the all but total capture of architecture within the capitalist 'hollow space' that makes 'true architecture' (and urbanism) impossible, as Bloch put it (Bloch, 1988 [1959]: 190).

Arguably, paralysed by its capture, architecture can do little more than re-inscribe alienation into the built environment as something of a repetition compulsion. In doing this, architecture largely elaborates on its own cultural irrelevance: characterised by social emptiness, or a general lack of ethical purpose beyond technocratic proficiency, economic reductionism or novel extravagance. Ironically, much of the source for the persisting irrelevance of architecture (and its theories) derives from the rejection of Utopia imagined by most adherents of the discipline as a necessary first step in responding to the failures of orthodox modern architecture and urban planning. Setting aside for a moment the common view of Utopia as all negative, re-valuing its generative potential reveals it as crucial for any attempt to imagine alternatives to existing conditions. In this regard, it is precisely the value Lefebvre ascribed to Utopia that makes him one of the most important twentieth-century thinkers on architecture and the city.

Setting aside for a moment the common view of Utopia as all negative, re-valuing its generative potential reveals it as crucial for any attempt to imagine alternatives to existing conditions.

It is with Utopia's potential and its banishment from architecture that the *cul-de-sac* of architectural theory in the present is revealed. Architects' developing anti-utopianism has, since the 1960s, seriously narrowed possibilities from within the discipline for asking searching questions about the ethical task of architecture and for piecing together answers. A good step forward would be to widen one's historical horizon, as Lefebvre does. Renaissance architect and theorist Leon Battista Alberti (1404–1472), for example, can begin to show the way. His treatise, *On the Art of Building*, is written as much, if not more, for patrons than for architects. His main objective throughout is to model a conception of right practice that both architect and client can aspire to, all within the social and architectural context of the city. Akin to Lefebvre, Alberti brings an extremely wide range of learning to bear on his topics.

However, there are other more contemporary theorists or practitioners from within architecture who can help to demonstrate Lefebvre's relevance for architects, two of whom are the Dutch architects Aldo van Eyck (1918–1999) and Herman Hertzberger (1932–). Van Eyck, in particular, can be put to work to illustrate Lefebvre's thinking for architects.

Van Eyck's anthropological approach to architecture and his conception of relativity parallels Lefebvre's own methodologies, especially with regard to how limited horizons of research and practice in architecture could be expanded. The central importance van Eyck gives to the social dimension and to the everyday, as the *loci* of potential, but also of conditions that limit possibility, associates him with Lefebvre. The two also share acknowledgement of the relevance of these factors to the production of space. The most explicit point of contact between Lefebvre and van Eyck is in the person of Dutch artist and architect Constant Nieuwenhuys (1920–2005), famous for his speculative New Babylon project, with whom van Eyck collaborated, and who Lefebvre was familiar with by way of his contact with the COBRA group of artists, and the Situationists (the group of social revolutionaries, made up of artists and intellectuals, active from 1957–1972, with whom Lefebvre was associated for a time). It is here that in a very real sense, Lefebvre's thinking comes into close proximity with architecture practice, albeit in some of its most unique forms (Bitter, Weber and Derksen 2009; Stanek 2011).

In much the way Utopia does, Lefebvre, as a thinker for architects, steadfastly returns social imagination to a politically neutered architecture which, out of habit as much as necessity, tends to operate in lockstep with the controlling narratives of capitalist realism. Moreover, Lefebvre's utopianism offers real and practical alternatives to the endgame of the Situationists (introduced above), the spatial limitations of Marxism (the foremost alternative system to capitalism), based on the political theories drawn from Karl Marx [1818–1883], which Lefebvre is most associated with, the pessimism of French postmodernist theorist Jean Baudrillard (1929–2007) (whose PhD thesis Lefebvre supervised), or Tafuri (who, though a Marxist historian, comes to very different conclusions than Lefebvre), and the claustrophobia of global capitalism (the apparent total social, political and economic system which now dominates).

The counter-practices suggested by Lefebvre that are outlined in what follows are proffered as alternatives to the commonplaces of conventional and less typical (so-called neo-avant-garde) architectural practices alike. In this regard, van Eyck's architecture, rather than Nieuwenhuys's New Babylon project, presents a clarifying counterform to Lefebvre's thinking on space, time and the city. Lefebvre's writing and van Eyck's architecture (and theory) still harbour radical implications for the invention of buildings and cities alike, even though the alternatives suggested by both have still been barely entered upon.

'Counter-practices', Amsterdam Orphanage, Amstelveenseweg, Amsterdam (1955–1960), Aldo van Eyck, Architect

Although the titles of Lefebvre's key writings on cities already translated into English have become shorthand for what is imagined to be the sum total of his key concepts – *The Right to the City, The Production of Space* and the *Critique of Everyday Life* – his expansion of Marxism and his utopianism are, after all, what unifies the myriad aspects of his project. However, one of the key aims of this book is to develop an understanding of how Lefebvre's contributions to contemporary architecture and urbanism could inform practice, thereby contributing to an understanding of him as well. In this sense, engagement with Lefebvre's thinking herein endeavours to elaborate on a *theory* for *practice* that is concrete enough to make imagining the interdependence of *formal closure* (of architecture) and *social processes* (of community) as core to the problem of inventing cities and buildings, while providing for their appropriation by individuals and groups (Harvey 2000). Emphasis on practical application – or at least relevance for it – in this discussion of Lefebvre, in relation to architecture and urbanism, highlights the concrete aspects of his theoretical discoveries.

In this sense, engagement with Lefebvre's thinking herein endeavours to elaborate on a *theory* for *practice* that is concrete enough to make imagining the interdependence of *formal closure* (of architecture) and *social processes* (of community) as core to the problem of inventing cities and buildings.

The very impossibility of inventing a 'true' architecture within the capitalist hollow space paradoxically becomes – or at least illuminates – *the very possibility* of how it might be possible to do just that. Beginning with the idea that the spaces we inhabit are so fully colonised by the market, and that subsequent spaces will be colonised by the same forces (from conception, to completion and inhabitation), the question of alternatives, as much as their prospect, would seem to turn in on itself, to implode under the pressure of those same forces that predetermine its capture within the panoptic sweep of the system – of the state and of capitalism. (Panoptic here refers – in a figurative way – to the prison designed by British social theorist Jeremy Bentham [1748–1832]. The prison he designed, called a Panopticon, was notable for its circular organisation of cells around a single point of observation that permitted one guard to keep an eye on all of the inmates. A further innovation of Bentham's panopticon was that the guard's station was shielded in such a way that he could observe the prisoners but they could not see him. Bentham believed that this arrangement would encourage prisoners to *internalise* the penal system represented by the all-seeing eyes of the guard and rehabilitate themselves. As used here, the *panoptic sweep of the system* refers to the pervasiveness of control associated with the dominant system of social, political and economic organisation, and the way individuals are encouraged to internalise the very omnipresence of the system by conforming to it.)

With the domination of everyday life – of work and organised consumption, and its spaces – by forces that can often feel total, alternatives can seem impossible. In turn, the apparent totality of the condition of impossibility, or inevitable defeat of any attempts to establish alternatives, arguably serves the aims of the system. If we come to believe that resistance is as impossible as escape or the reinvention of *what is*, then survival might seem to leave no option other than surrender to *the given*. Under such conditions, only acquiescence, or dreams of some far off, though improbable, revolution, offers the illusion of agency or liberation. And yet, in Lefebvre's view, it is also – at least potentially – the landscape of the everyday out of which change can arise, but not before the everyday is subjected to a sustained critique, revealing at one and the same time the collusion of everyday life with the forces that dominate it, and those aspects of it that continue to exist under the radar, or beyond the reach, of the dominant world system. In point of fact, narratives of totality, whether they come from within the system (and promote the view that *there is no alternative* to it), or emerge from its edges (and convincingly argue that *it is easier to imagine the end of the world* than it is to imagine alternatives to the very system ostensibly being resisted), only serve to obscure the cracks that inevitably form in the apparent monolith of *what is*. It is in this regard that Lefebvre emerges as the *philosopher of cracks*, in much the way Bloch is the *philosopher of hope*.

Lefebvre did not shy away from confronting the social, economic, political and habitual realities of *the given*, or the forces that shape and sustain the status quo. Rather, he recognised each of these forces as contributing to the shape of conditions that can appear both total and permanent. In this sense, practices (architectural, social, cultural, political) can never be autonomous, but are rather conditioned by the systems that – at least in part – determine the consciousness that imagines and enacts the practices which reproduce those very same systems. Obviously, architecture and urbanism are as predetermined by this process as are other social activities. As the system becomes naturalised in people's consciousness through the rehearsal of habits and social rituals in its settings, attempts to locate the untimely openings out of which other possibilities might materialise are apparently nullified. But unlike theorists of total closure, such as Tafuri or Jameson, Lefebvre did not believe that the world system is ever quite as absolute as it might appear.

However, even if Lefebvre believed that his critiques of everyday life could identify those corners of existence not yet fully colonised by the system, he was aware that architects' dependence on the patronage of that very system renders them – compared with other artists or professionals – singularly ill equipped to make sustained critiques of *what is*, of the sort that might actually disclose possibilities beyond simply more novel results. In fact, Lefebvre opens up routes towards making possible the imagination of settings that dignify the complexity of human existence, and which provide social spaces for the emergence of seemingly impossible alternatives.

Lefebvre and architecture

The first chapter of this book offers a partial overview of Lefebvre's body of work, with an emphasis on his reworking of Romanticism and Utopia in relation to architecture. Crisscrossing Lefebvre's work with this emphasis has two primary aims: first, to highlight the importance of both in his thinking. And second, to articulate how these developments suggest the outlines of alternative architectural and urban practices; in particular by building upon Lefebvre's critique of architects' habits of representation in conceptualisations of space.

In Chapter 2 the focus turns to what is perhaps Lefebvre's most important and influential work, *The Production of Space*, in which he develops a history of space, showing how it becomes a product under state capitalism and globalisation and how, in this shift, spaces lose much of their value as a setting for social life.

A close reading of *The Production of Space* is central to the aims of this book partly because of its importance for the development of so-called radical geography since its first publication but also for its relevance to deepening conceptualisations of architectural problems. However, architects' general lack of interest in social and political problems ensures the reproduction of neoliberal spaces of consumption now, and into the foreseeable future as well. It is worth noting that *The Production of Space*, which was originally published in 1974, came out when Lefebvre was already in his seventies. As such, the book is a culmination of his lifelong engagement with the problems of modernity and the modern city that parallels the rise and fall of communism in Russia, from the 1917 Revolution to the fall of the Berlin Wall in 1989, and the demise of the Soviet Union in 1991, just six months after Lefebvre's death.

The sweep of Lefebvre's life and of his interests and writing offers a remarkable roadmap to the twentieth century, and thus remains suggestive for the twenty-first as well. Never far from Lefebvre's interests is his persistent rethinking of Marxism; more precisely, the enduring value of Marx's conceptualisations of social relations for a critique of capitalism, and even of globalisation. But Marx's work, fixed at the moment of the emergence of his ideas, proved unsatisfactory for Lefebvre, not least because the gaps in Marx's thinking, with reference to the city and to space, called for an extension to his ideas. With this in mind, and in consideration of architecture culture in the West, it is safe to say that the most significant exclusion in architecture education and practice is Marx as an *aide–mémoire* for thinking through the apparently intractable problems confronting architecture in our age, variously described as a crisis of meaning, of ideology, or the (im)possibility of architecture under the conditions of global capitalism.

The most significant exclusion in architecture education and practice is Marx as an *aide–mémoire* for thinking through the apparently intractable problems confronting architecture in our age.

Marx has on occasion found a way into architecture through the side door in the writing of Tafuri, most importantly in his *Architecture and Utopia: Design and Capitalist Development* (originally published in 1973), in the work of Kenneth Frampton, in his *Modern Architecture: A Critical History* (first published in 1980), and somewhat less directly in geographer David Harvey's *Spaces of Hope* (2000) and *Rebel Cities* (2012), which are, in many ways, homages to Lefebvre and Marx. Jameson's understanding of architecture under postmodern conditions articulates an intersection between Marx and Utopia, showing also the influence of Lefebvre. The Frankfurt School casts Marx's shadow on architecture by way of its influence on theory, primarily in the figures of Walter Benjamin, Theodor Adorno and Ernst Bloch. And yet, in almost every instance when these authors, including Lefebvre, are included on reading lists, or are held up as suggesting how a design might be conceptualised, the Marxian dimension of their thinking is excised (almost always along with the utopian).

The third and final chapter of this study of Lefebvre for architects offers a close reading of *Rhythmanalysis: Space, Time and Everyday Life*, which is Lefebvre's last book. In its English version, first published in translation in 2004, Lefebvre's writings on the topic are collected, including the longer *Elements of Rhythmanalysis: An Introduction to the Understanding of Rhythms*, first published in 1992, the year following Lefebvre's death, as well as shorter pieces first published in 1985 and 1987 and written with his last wife, Catherine Régulier. While the book is literally the culmination of Lefebvre's life's work for being his last, it is also a capstone inasmuch as it is a remarkably lucid evocation of a method for becoming alive to what is, or ought to be, the object of architects' interests and designs: the lived city and social life, in all of their spatial and temporal richness. *Elements of Rhythmanalysis* is also the final elaboration of the method of analysis developed by Lefebvre in *The Production of Space*. As such, like the earlier book, it contains much that will be of interest to architects.

Although keen readers of Lefebvre will likely have much to quarrel with me about over which aspects of his corpus I have chosen to include, as much as with what I have decided to set aside, in the context of this present book at least, my aim has been to try and give an overview of Lefebvre's ideas without doing too much violence to them through reduction, which would have been a betrayal of not just the atmosphere of his thought but of his convictions as well: amongst the many sins of capitalism, reductionism is, for Lefebvre, arguably the most pervasive and nefarious. Thus, in an attempt to avoid trading the depth and breadth of Lefebvre's thought for some superficial appropriation or banal commoditisation of it, I have determined that treating less in more depth is closer to the spirit of Lefebvre than a short summary of more of it would have been. After all, Lefebvre wrote more than sixty books; attempting to introduce more than a very select few of them in any depth in as short a book as this one is just not possible.

An associated issue is the problem of demonstrating the relevance of Lefebvre for architects. The greatest risk in attempting this is that of instrumentalising Lefebvre's thinking, transforming it into a *hammer* rather than valuing it as a *lever*, for its generative capacities. The pitfall of instrumentalisation is a common one in attempts to make use of ideas external to architecture within it, particularly in relation to design and practice.

The business necessity of architecture limits practitioners' capacity for social and political imagination. Ultimately, most architecture constructed today simply reconfirms that *there is no alternative*, no possible future outside the system. Even putatively radical, critical or avant-garde, or neo-avant-garde, works of architecture generally succeed only in confirming the near total capture of the building industry within the hollow space of global capitalism. Indeed, the apparent totality of the current prevailing social, economic and political system can make alternatives seem unimaginable (as Tafuri believed). However, such pessimism is also a necessary and generative first step: acknowledging the apparently all-encompassing nature of the system intensifies desires for alternatives. This paradox is rendered in Lefebvre's thinking as the 'possible impossible', that which appears out of the question only if the present moment is taken to be eternal.

For Lefebvre, a major route out of the apparently impossible is to look to the past for alternatives to the present, and to identify tentative openings in the present giving access to other futures. The key setting where past and present intersect is the everyday. Critique of the everyday also reveals subtle forms of resistance and subversion that can enliven imagination. And yet, every counterproposal can appear as if it has already been captured by the system it ostensibly acts against (even the very possibility of alternatives might serve as proof of the system's largesse). But what if it is only in such moments of deep

14   INTRODUCTION

'Everyday Life: New York City in the 1970s'

despair that the imagination can be shaken enough to conceive of possibilities beyond the limiting confines of the system?

Architecture thinking its own thoughts

The *Thinkers for Architects* series of which this present volume is part suggests two things worth considering (in particular alongside Lefebvre): one is that architecture is a discipline with its own way of knowing, hence, *Thinkers for Architects*, rather than simply *Thinkers* (for anyone / everyone). And, two, architecture's lack of confidence in its status as a discipline makes the moves beyond the discipline of architecture that characterises the volumes in this series (including this one), inevitable if not necessary. At its most troubling, this suggests that, although architecture is still conceived of as a distinct discipline, it has great difficulty *thinking its own thoughts*, not least out of the tradition of its own (theoretical) literature and past practices. Oddly, the difficulty, or inability, to think its own thoughts has become ever more pronounced for architecture during the years which might be characterised by the 'theory boom' in architecture that began in the 1970s.

The paradox of *Thinkers for Architects* thinking thoughts for architects, or with them, but only from outside of architecture, and the inverse relation between the theory explosion in architecture and the declining influence of its own earlier literature, highlights the crisis in architecture culture identified by Tafuri, the endgame of which is either that architecture is no longer a discipline in its own right or that it will inevitably disappear in any traditional or historical sense, again as Tafuri observed.

But therein lies a further paradox: if architecture now requires thinkers from outside of the discipline to be able to think its thoughts, that might actually herald the potential for disciplinary renewal, largely because architects have mostly forgotten how to think as architects from within the discipline, or have abandoned the possibility of doing so, and so now require the assistance of non-architects to help them to recollect how to think for themselves. Thus, pressing non-architects into service, as thinkers for architects, need not be nearly as pessimistic, or self-abnegating, as it might at first seem. My aim in this book is to make Lefebvre *speak to architects* by showing how he *speaks like an architect*, or at least like a reconstituted thinker of architecture able to think his own thoughts; able to think beyond the crisis of architecture foisted upon it by capitalism, which the general lack of disciplinary self-confidence – which is a symptom – exacerbates.

My aim in this book is to make Lefebvre *speak to architects* by showing how he *speaks like an architect*, or at least like a reconstituted thinker of architecture able to think his own thoughts; able to think beyond the crisis of architecture foisted upon it by capitalism.

In the chapters that follow, I will introduce architects to a Lefebvre who could help them to think their own thoughts, independently. To achieve this, Lefebvre must first be claimed by architects from geographers, sociologists and cultural theorists alike, but without alienating those crucial thinkers for architects, and hopefully keeping their interest as well. To achieve this, an act of translation, as much as of interpretation or transposition, is required. In most studies of Lefebvre he speaks like a sociologist, or is made to speak to sociologists or geographers, rather than speaking like, or to, architects, whose own ways of knowing and doing are nonetheless perpetually renewed and fortified by being opened to the influence of myriad other disciplines, in much the way Lefebvre's own method was enriched by multiple influences. Indeed, all this, paradoxically, so that architects might begin to imagine how they could think their own thoughts (again).

CHAPTER 2

Utopia and a new Romanticism

In naming what is involved in utopia as method, I mean to encourage and endorse this as a legitimate and useful mode of thought and knowledge generation. Utopia as method is not and cannot be blueprint. Utopian envisioning is necessarily provisional, reflexive and dialogic. [. . .] The utopian alternative is to think where we might want to get to and what routes are open to us. But if we know that our hopes for the future are indicative projections of what might be, we know too that these are always coloured by the conditions of generation. The social imaginary, including its image of potential futures, is always the imaginary generated by a particular society.

(Levitas 2013: 218–219)

Utopia as the prospect of the possible

In our times, it can seem as though there really is no alternative to the way things are, which makes it especially difficult to imagine possibilities beyond the already achievable. But, as is explored in this chapter, Lefebvre reminds us that venturing beyond the given only appears impossible. He consistently alerts us to the illusory compensations of making-do with reality. Ultimately, a rational and quantifying mind-set has grown up alongside the increasing dominance of global capitalism, which together severely limit the horizons of possibility. Although accepting limitations may seem a hard-won achievement of rationality, it will be an empty accomplishment if it extinguishes hope or desire. Even if reaching beyond the present almost always ends in frustration, disabling utopian longing as a way to be *free* of inevitable disappointment threatens to leave the future without a project. The evident dreariness of resignation surrounds us; in the seemingly inevitable blighting of the built environment; in increasingly unequal societies; in the marketisation of education; and in the transformation of citizens into consumers. Perhaps these discouraging developments, which were always the focus of Lefebvre's critique, can be best summed up by the philosophical system of *positivism*, which recognises only scientific explanation and logical or mathematical proof, and therefore must reject anything that proving of this sort cannot account for – Utopia and Romanticism, for example. Although no panacea, without the idea of Utopia the future has no shape; and without the past, Utopia has no content.

Rather than anticipating life, architecture often provides settings that could only function as planned had the architect also designed the inhabitants. With fewer and fewer exceptions, this is the prevailing condition of architecture and modernity. The rise and fall of positivism is at the root of this, chronicling the drama of architecture throughout the twentieth century. In the event, the brave new world of architectural and urban modernism, articulated, for example, by architectural historian and CIAM (*Congrès International d'Architecture Moderne*) Secretary Sigfried Giedion (1888–1968), has rarely taken flesh, except in degenerate form (Giedion 1982). It is precisely the empty promises, false hopes and extravagant failures of modernist architecture and urbanism that preoccupied Lefebvre in much of his writing.

By the late 1940s, the so-called utopian architecture of modernity, identified (mostly inaccurately) with Le Corbusier and (somewhat more accurately) with CIAM, emerged as the official architectural style for most governments, institutions, corporations and cities (Coleman 2005, 2007, 2012a, 2013a; Giedion 1982: 696–706). Achievement of this status revealed the putatively rebellious architecture of utopian promise – associated with the first half of the twentieth century – as mostly incapable of touching emotion; a disappointing outcome for an ideal built largely upon the nineteenth-century Christian utopian, and utopian socialist, reform visions of John Ruskin (1818–1900) and William Morris (1834–1896), amongst others (Coleman 2005, 2008). Yet, rather than confirming the dead end of Utopia, nineteenth-century utopian socialism and Romanticism could rescue modernity from being simply an object of criticism by recollecting its promise. Indeed, it is on this paradoxical foundation that Lefebvre constructs a positive utopian prospect for architecture and the city, which also sets a challenge to the bad name of Utopia and Romanticism.

In what follows, I explore the trajectory of utopian promise for Lefebvre, against a contemporary backdrop where Utopia is mostly anathema for architects (and laypeople). To fully appreciate the richness of Lefebvre's dialectical and experimental utopianism, it is necessary to begin with his engagement with the past, with Romanticism, and how this is key to his important contributions to the development of the concept of Utopia as method. ('Dialectical' refers to a method of inquiry and analysis characterised by the consideration of apparently incompatible [opposite and contradictory] concepts in an attempt to reveal misunderstandings of them, and to work towards resolution of disagreements between them, potentially generating new, more robust, concepts that reconcile tensions between them without rejecting this tension.)

To fully appreciate the richness of Lefebvre's dialectical and experimental utopianism, it is necessary to begin with his engagement with the past, with Romanticism.

Romanticism and Utopia

Arguably, Lefebvre's thinking is cognate with the transformative and critical visions of nineteenth-century British utopian and Christian Socialists, in particular Ruskin and Morris. Establishing the association of Lefebvre with these earlier thinkers reveals his project as both a continuation of and an elaboration on their insights (Coleman 2005; Frampton 2007: 42–50). Most obviously, Ruskin and Morris were as preoccupied with architecture and the city as they were with social and artistic reform. Their writing forges an indissoluble link between the organisation and appearance of the city and the kind of life it might foster and sustain. It is in the revelation and amplification of the unshakable bond between aesthetics and ethics – between the conditions of production and what is produced – that Lefebvre is most akin to Ruskin and Morris.

Associating Lefebvre with Ruskin and Morris sheds light on the intersection between Romanticism – as a critique of modernity made from the distance of a pre-modern position – and Utopia – conceptualised as anticipating a Not Yet, or possible-impossible conditions, achievable sometime in the future, built upon reform efforts in the present (Löwy and Sayre 2001: 1–56, 222–225; Shields 1999: 73):

> **In reality, this bond with the Romantic tradition is one of the sources of the originality – indeed, the singularity – of Lefebvre's thought in the historical panorama of French Marxism, [which was] marked from the outset by the insidious and permanent presence of positivism. Throughout Lefebvre's entire intellectual itinerary, his reflection continued to be enriched by a confrontation with Romanticism.**
>
> **(Löwy and Sayre 2001: 223)**

That Lefebvre, as a radical and progressive thinker, looked backwards – if not exactly to a golden age then at least to a pre-modern, pre-industrial and thus pre-capitalist organisation of production and individual and social life – with analogous expression in the form and character of the city, will only surprise if one has undue faith in progress.

Lefebvre's looking backwards was neither retrograde nor reactionary. Nor did it entail a rejection of industrial progress and modernity. Rather, it ensured that his imagining of possible alternatives, and the pathways to them, had a solid foundation in the achievements of the past. As such, past and future intermingle in his thinking: 'His goal is to transcend the limits of the old Romanticism and establish the foundation for a new Romanticism, a revolutionary Romanticism oriented toward the future' (Löwy and Sayre 2001: 223). A utopian register for Romanticism made it possible for Lefebvre to work towards alternative conditions based on prior experiences, but free of nostalgia for some impossible return to origins. It is worth noting that, although Lefebvre is best known for his work on cities, his earliest research was focused on rural sociology in transition from pre-capitalist to capitalist production, and the negative effects of these transformations on community life. Throughout his life, he maintained an interest in the relationship between city and country. When Lefebvre's focus shifted from the country to the town, he retained the social and spatial organisation of rural pre-capitalist conditions as the source of his critique of capitalist space.

Despite the words *romantic* and *utopian* commonly signifying an unhealthy attachment to some alternative apparently impossibly located out of physical or temporal reach, confluence of the two in Lefebvre's thought was generative of his far-ranging social critique of modernity. As such, Lefebvre introduces the specific potential of overcoming modernism with a particular sort of postmodernism, which promises more responsive and just social settings. Understood in this way, the postmodern (as coming after – and out of – modernity) offers something potentially far more substantial and liberating than the historicist trifles of stylistic postmodernist architecture that have dominated the remaking of cities since at least the 1980s. It also avoids the parallel notion that overcoming all-encompassing explanations (or master-narratives) of reality, of the sort associated with the overconfidence of modernity, must inevitably reveal radical subjectivity and extreme, near paralytic, relativism as the only viable alternatives.

Rather than deploying spurious images of the past in the present, or overindulging in present-day fashions, the postmodern theorised by Lefebvre is not exhausted by the decline of modernity. Instead, his co-mingling of Utopia and Romanticism offers a way out of the cul-de-sac of an insecure present. By introducing a capacity for imagining alternatives to the limited and limiting perspectives of capitalism, and the constraints this places upon individual and social life and the city as their setting, Lefebvre's holistic critical method – simultaneously utopian and romantic – effectively reveals the relationship between social and architectural forms, including the economic and spatial conditions out of which they arise.

Although not typically attended to by architects, social and spatial arrangements are manifestations of particular systems of organisation, which they also express. Such interrelationships inevitably affect the morphology of social and spatial relations on domestic and civic levels as well. Thus, despite all its wonders of bustle, the transparency and alienation of the modern city is nothing less than a framework that analogises capitalist production and consumption as it facilitates both. Hence, Lefebvre argues that substantive social reform necessarily requires correlate spatial reform. However, much as the two are inseparable, genuine social and spatial reform will only be possible if the systems that actually organise both are subjected to radical critique. Revealing the matrix (or substructure and infrastructure) underpinning the superstructure of evident social and spatial reality is the first step to reworking what exists, though there are many obstacles to achieving this:

Lefebvre argues that substantive social reform necessarily requires correlate spatial reform. However, much as the two are inseparable, genuine social and spatial reform will only be possible if the systems that actually organise both are subjected to radical critique.

> In connection with the city and its extensions (outskirts, suburbs) one occasionally hears talk of a 'pathology of space' of 'ailing neighbourhoods' and so on. This kind of phraseology makes it easy for people who use it – architects, urbanists, planners – to suggest the idea that they are in effect 'doctors of space'. This is to promote the spread of some particularly mystifying notions, and especially the idea that the modern city is a product not of the capitalist or neocapitalist system but rather of some putative 'sickness' of society. Such formulations serve to divert attention from the criticism of space to replace critical analysis by schemata that are at once not very rational and very reactionary. Taken to their logical limits, these theses can deem society as a whole and 'man' as a social being to be sicknesses of nature.
>
> (Lefebvre 1991 [1974]: 99)

Almost all attempts to remake the city are informed by just the sorts of diversions indicated earlier. Conceptualising cities as diseased organisms that make society sick presupposes that they can only be cured by radical surgery as something necessary for protecting citizens. Ultimately, this mind-set effectively avoids confronting the underlying systems of organisation that actually produce the apparent morbidity of city and society. The bizarre habit of demolishing large swaths of cities by choice in the name of progress, economic development or even apparent necessity (a cure) mirrors capitalism's vocation for constant activity and change, and attendant alienation, necessary for it to function and survive (Harvey 2000).

Urban surgery of the sort that is imposed from above and radically transforms the physical character of cities actually displaces the very reform it is meant to achieve even further from the realm of real possibility. But if most contemporary architecture and remade cities are alienating, it is not simply because architectural education is tragically flawed, or that architecture students and graduates are incompetent, or even that clients (public or private) are philistine

'A Sick City? London in the 1970s' (view toward Nicholas Hawksmoor's Christ Church Spitalfields, 1714–1729)

and the authorities charged with assuring the quality and benefits of new development are irrecoverably corrupt. Rather, because we are each born into the dominant system of our given context, and imperceptibly inculcated into it, the limits of possibility are largely determined by the consciousness produced by our social conditions. In this way, in large part, we can only imagine what is already imaginable and possible, and can construct only that which reproduces the values of the system within which we build. Perhaps reproduction of this sort would be acceptable if the system into which one is inculcated were benign or better, though it is more troubling if that system is brutal or unequal (Lefebvre 1991 [1974]). Renewal projects innocent of strategies for reforming the underlying sources of the existing conditions they are meant to transform will likely accomplish little more than 'rattling the cage'. Considering such prerequisites for change, substantial reform could appear to be forever out of reach. However, Lefebvre's holistic provocations for change offer a different conclusion: his circular dialectical process makes it possible to test the limits of possibility. Ultimately, social reform presupposes spatial reform, as spatial reform presupposes social reform; proven by the persistent failure of totalising urban renewal projects and social housing schemes that are mostly implemented without the benefit of research or testing.

The instability of such so-called urban innovations reveals their primarily decorative character in the sense that they enhance (rather than critique) the underlying system of which they are inevitably expressions. The near total capture of architecture by the cultural logic of late capitalism led German philosopher of hope, Ernst Bloch, to declare that architecture and urban planning are unpromising vehicles for gaining access to the 'Not Yet' that Utopia opens vistas on to. According to him, capitalism permeates both so fully that: 'Only the beginnings of a different society will make true architecture possible again' (Bloch 1959: 186–190).

Generate and degenerate Utopias

Lefebvre's reference to the social and spatial forms of the pre-modern and pre-industrial city is a means for critiquing the modern (capitalist) city. It is surely not, as Harvey believes, a cul-de-sac in which possibilities are turned in on themselves. Nor does it foreclose on potentialities or alternatives. Harvey may make a negative diagnosis of Lefebvre's referencing of past cities but Lefebvre's aim in doing so was, above all else, generative (Harvey 2000: 183). Even so, Harvey's reservations are worth considering. While he correctly observes that 'Lefebvre is resolutely antagonistic to the traditional utopianisms of spatial form precisely because of their closed authoritarianism [traditional class and gender roles, for example]' and that '[h]e fashions a devastating critique of Cartesian conceptions, of the political absolutism [totalitarianism, tyranny, authoritarianism] that flows from absolute conceptions of space, of the oppressions visited upon the world by a rationalized, bureaucratized, technocratically, and capitalistically-defined spatiality', he finds Lefebvre's apparent unwillingness to propose concrete solutions exasperating (Harvey 2000: 183). However, he is even more suspicious of Lefebvre's Romanticism:

> For him, the production of space must always remain an endlessly open possibility. The effect unfortunately, is to leave the actual spaces of any alternative frustratingly undefined. Lefebvre refuses specific recommendations (though there are some nostalgic hints that they got it right in Renaissance Tuscany). He refuses to confront the underlying problem: that to materialize a space is to engage in closure (however temporary) which is an authoritarian act. [. . .] [T]he problem of closure [. . .] cannot be endlessly evaded. To do so is to embrace an agonistic [combative, though futile] romanticism of perpetually unfulfilled longing and desire.
>
> (Harvey 2000: 182–183)

Lefebvre's apparent aversion to authoritarianism, to proposing concrete spatial forms which echo renewed forms of social (or everyday) life, momentarily avoids the inevitable entrapment of architects and planners within the dominant system; a reasonable condition, at least until a transformed consciousness takes shape. In the interim, Lefebvre's reluctance to recommend a particular form of spatial closure is pragmatic: any particular prescription for the new city could, as Harvey observes, only be provisional anyway. Harvey's impatience aside, Lefebvre understands that imagining new spatial forms that analogise and support renewed social forms and processes is much more difficult than imagining those new social forms in the first place. By refusing to engage in seemingly authoritarian acts of closure, Lefebvre avoids the pitfalls of a sort of operative criticism which tends to shift quickly from theoretical concerns to matters of style, or formal preference.

Lefebvre's apparent aversion to authoritarianism, to proposing concrete spatial forms which echo renewed forms of social (or everyday) life, momentarily avoids the inevitable entrapment of architects and planners within the dominant system; a reasonable condition, at least until a transformed consciousness takes shape.

Because design and construction are so thoroughly determined by the limiting perspectives of the present – by the seemingly eternal given of capitalist realism – attempts to act outside of such constraints are quickly neutralised by the very process of realisation (Fisher 2009). In lieu of fantastical mental images of new spatial forms for a renewed city and social life, Lefebvre recollected pre-capitalist modes of life and production which offered a pathway for recuperating forms of individual and social life in the present; conversely, modernity unhinged from the past is destructive:

> in ancient rural communities [. . .], a certain human fulfilment was to be found – albeit mingled with disquiet and the seeds of all the agonies to come. That fulfilment has since disappeared. [. . .] The result for our rural areas has been a deprivation of everyday life on a vast scale. [. . .] Bit by bit everything which formerly contributed to the splendour of everyday life [. . .] has been stripped from it and made to appear as something beyond

its own self. Progress has been *real, and in certain aspects immense*, but it has been dearly paid. [. . .] Rural areas tell us above all of the dislocation of primitive community, of poor technical progress, of the decline of a way of life which is much less different from that of ancient times than is generally believed. Towns tell us of the almost total decomposition of community, the atomization of society into 'private' individuals.

(Lefebvre 2008 [1947/1958]: 209, 210, 229, 233)

The tension between progress and its cost – in terms of the loss of 'the splendour of everyday life' – Lefebvre establishes in this sequence of quotes illustrates his engagement with the past: what it offers him, and why it is worth considering. The easiest way to understand the loss Lefebvre laments is to reflect on all of the divisions that capitalism entails, from the division of labour, to the increasing separations between producer and consumer, life and work, urban and rural, and within communities themselves. In Lefebvre's terms, this all equates to alienation, to the loss of a more directly lived and experienced life, which carries with it great social and individual costs in terms of a wide range of social and individual associations.

Because Lefebvre's Romanticism concentrates on what has been lost and, by way of inversion, what might be regained in the future, albeit in an as yet indeterminate form, Harvey's charge that Lefebvre's 'romanticism' was an 'agonistic' rejection of the present that goes nowhere except towards 'perpetually unfulfilled longing and desire' appears to neglect just how generative 'unfulfilled longing and desire' can be. Pursuing this further, it is worth noting that Lefebvre goes beyond just 'some nostalgic hints that they got it right in Renaissance Tuscany'. Indeed, he confirms this in a concise expression of his praise for Florence: 'My favourite city is Florence which has ceased recently to be a mummified city, a museum city, and which has found again an activity, thanks to the small modern industries of the periphery' (Lefebvre 1986: 208). Lefebvre deftly communicates here a preoccupation with tradition and modernity alike and with cities that are vital, rather than being either preserved in aspic or overwhelmed by the progress of modernity. Of particular importance for architects is the way Lefebvre stands expectation on its head: he upends the conventional association of technological progress with social progress, revealing the first as potentially destructive, with the second requiring engagement with alternatives (residing in the past) to capitalism and modernity's solvent aspects. Thought of in this way, the past is radical precisely because it is closer to the roots of culture.

Florence, Italy, *Centro Storico* (2000). Activity by the Uffizi Gallery (1560–1581)

Ultimately, Lefebvre's unwillingness to 'materialize a space or engage in closure' posits the specifics of renewed spatial form as an open question to be resolved in each instance. The first steps to reform will likely come from non-specialist citizens undeterred by professional restrictions who demand a different space and begin to make it themselves. If new spatial forms must be preceded by the new social forms out of which they could emerge, there are two possible outcomes: either architecture will be impossible until society changes first; or, because architecture is socially constructed, it need not worry too much about that which it has little or no influence upon – politics or society. However, here again Lefebvre posits an inversion: what if a new life must actually be preceded by a new space? The implication of this for the way the task of architecture is generally understood is significant. The full implications of this apparently counterintuitive assertion challenge the conclusions of most histories and theories of architecture developed since the 1960s.

Taken together, the potent mixture of reform-minded idealism and optimism about the perfectibility of individual, state and place – as suggested by Utopia and Romanticism – could fortify a stubborn impracticality that holds out the promise of shattering the bonds of restrictive realism. In the context of Lefebvre's thought, Romanticism is a kind of utopian anticipation enriched by the residue of unfinished alternatives blown forward from the past. In this regard, Lefebvre arguably recognises in the past its uncompleted work, in the form of what Marx described as a 'mystical consciousness which is still unclear to itself' (Marx 1843, quoted in Bloch 1959: 155–156). Analysis of this obscure, or as yet unintelligible, consciousness – percolating up from the past – might well reveal 'that the world has long possessed the dream of a matter, of which it must only possess consciousness in order to possess it in reality' (Marx 1843, quoted in Bloch 1959: 156). In his historiography of space and in his considerations of pre-capitalist social arrangements, Lefebvre attempts to grasp this consciousness as part of a Utopian method to make dreams real.

The dream of which Marx writes correlates with Ernst Bloch's conception of *Concrete Utopia*, which manifests the anticipatory function of hope by directing thought and action towards achieving the *Real-Possible* (as opposed to what Bloch called the fruitless *Empty-Possible* of *Abstract-Utopias*, like the empty formalism of some architectural modernisms, that seem *compensatory* rather than *anticipatory*). Anticipation of achievable alternatives begins with clarifying the 'mystical consciousness' of the past that persists into the present precisely because it remains unfulfilled. When reclaimed, such consciousness becomes a first concrete step towards transforming what is anticipated into reality. Not surprisingly, Bloch's conception of the *Real-Possible* and Lefebvre's *Possible-Impossible* are very close in spirit to one another. However, Lefebvre's inclusion of 'impossible' actually brings his ideas closer to the real situation, in which attempts to exceed (or overcome) the limits of the given are rejected as unachievable as a matter of course, whether or not achievement is only impossible in this moment. In any event, Lefebvre's *Possible-Impossible* can only touch consciousness to become potentially achievable if 'the thoughts of the past' are carried through, which presumes a fluid, dialectical process, rather than some fixed blueprint-like schema (Marx 1843, quoted in Bloch 1959: 156).

Lefebvre's Romanticism was not nostalgic in a conventional sense. For example, because return is 'both impossible and inconceivable', any wholesale 'return to the past' does not hold out any promise of resolving the 'crisis of modernity'. And yet he observed that even if '[t]owns have always been collective works of art', new towns 'are born of ugliness and boredom', which renders them unsatisfactory (Lefebvre 1995 [1962]: 279). Although the past is impossible to recover, Lefebvre's awareness that earlier (pre-modern) towns embody something that new towns do not could be of benefit to architects. By accepting the tension between the value of the past and its inaccessible distance, Lefebvre establishes a dialectical relationship between earlier towns and contemporary ones: traditional arrangements offer a way to think beyond the limited and unsatisfying prospects of modern conditions without falling into a nostalgic trap. Despite its frequent disappointments, the modern is the inescapable context of our lives and thus is also the locus of our possibilities. Escape is not an option, and alternatives may be immanent, or latent, in the past, but resolution to the crisis of modernity, of contemporary towns, is not immediately within reach:

> **Can the people who populate them, who live in them, who shape them according to their needs, also create them, or will that remain the prerogative of the small group which plans, builds and organizes them? Up until now the answer has been no, and this failure is the crucial problem.**
>
> (Lefebvre 1995 [1962]: 279)

Arguably, the failings of modern towns and the promise of past ones are largely self-evident. Nevertheless, achieving a concrete synthesis, resulting in superior alternatives, remains difficult. In the quote just cited, Lefebvre sets involvement in shaping a town from its creation – 'according to their needs' – by the people who live there, against the dominion of a small group of specialists (planners, architects and bureaucrats) who are primarily responsible for conceiving and constructing towns, and for spreading the ugly, boring and alienating conditions of the modern built environment. Although self-determination in making towns is difficult to imagine, Lefebvre introduces it as an alternative worth considering.

The apparent ebbing of beauty in the modern world – ugly and boring towns are an example – concerned Lefebvre. The modern sense of aesthetic appreciation or sensual delight alone was not his interest; instead, for him, beauty is a kind of comprehensiveness. As he puts it: 'Is this not the problem of harmony again, but renewed in another context, the practical context of full and active participation in everyday life, and with a different meaning to the one it has in relation to art and aesthetics taken in isolation?' (Lefebvre 1995 [1962]: 279). Clearly, Lefebvre's preoccupation with the built environment is primarily social and comprehensive. However, his debt to the past is also worth noting, in this instance to earlier ways of conceptualising beauty as made up of eurhythmically interrelated parts (suggesting the rhythmic and proportional interrelationship of individual parts – of bodies, societies or forms – to one another and to the whole, which they form), largely drawn from the first-century BC Roman architect and theorist, Vitruvius (Bk. I, Ch. II, p. 14).

32   UTOPIA AND A NEW ROMANTICISM

The apparent ebbing of beauty in the modern world – ugly and boring towns are an example – concerned Lefebvre. The modern sense of aesthetic appreciation or sensual delight alone was not his interest; instead, for him, beauty is a kind of comprehensiveness.

Critiques of everyday life

In Lefebvre's view, the everyday has been deformed through its increasing colonisation by positivism – in the intensifying rigid organisation of life and work, and their settings. Suppression of the quotidian (or habitual) to bureaucracy – such as prevails today – inevitably increases disunity in community life by spreading alienation. In contrast, Lefebvre proposed a unitary theory of the everyday. Although critical of the excesses of nineteenth-century Romanticism, Lefebvre embraced its critique of bourgeois life. Romanticism's aptitude for acting against the destructive forces of modernity through clarifying distanciation – the 'otherness' of an ideal, unified, pre-capitalist past – is also key. By emphasising these crucial aspects of Romanticism, Lefebvre could project a forward-looking Revolutionary Romanticism capable of shaping the prospect of an alternative future of a reunified everyday unbound by a specific idealised past.

Although Lefebvre's critical project was fortified by the generative tensions between past and future, his ultimate goal was a reunified, disalienated society. For him, capitalism and alienation are interwoven, in much the way that inequality and the dissolution of everyday life are symptomatic of both. According to Lefebvre, only the return of some unity to everyday life and its spaces can overcome alienation. In his view, the most obvious way to achieve this is to renew social and spatial conditions by reimagining pre-modern conditions that predate capitalism and alienation. Ultimately, the spatial correlates of disalienation are settings that could contain and sustain a convivial everyday life in all dimensions and at every scale. Inevitably, Lefebvre's idea that a radical and generative past is necessary for the formation of a reconstituted alternative future – characterised by a vital social life and its spatial frame – runs contrary to almost all myths of progress and modernity. In this regard, he believed that for the *possible impossible* to take (its as yet undetermined) shape, it must be built upon the recollected memories of unified moments projected forward from a past (that once was, or that had been partially achieved) into the future as a *not-yet*.

Lefebvre's conviction that transformation is always a possibility charts a way beyond the limitations of Marx, the cul-de-sac of total closure presented by Tafuri, or the proliferation of neoliberal and global capitalist spatial practices in shaping the built environment and social life. Nevertheless, by moving beyond the limitations of thinking the future in terms of revolution or progress, Lefebvre's ideas are set against the practice habits of architects, planners and urban designers, which makes it difficult for such professionals to translate his discoveries into their working methods.

There is no alternative? Or, Lefebvre and Utopia

Turning from Lefebvre's radical Romanticism, the discussion now shifts towards a consideration of his dialectical and experimental utopianism, which – in tandem with his Romanticism – significantly expands horizons of possibility for imagining and realising alternatives. Lefebvre's utopian practice suggests how architects and planners might recuperate their capacities for establishing settings where the everyday can flourish, beyond reproducing the neoliberal city. Despite an increasing Anglo-American awareness of Lefebvre's work, urban and architectural practices have not deepened much since he wrote on cities. One reason for this is that the student revolts and general strikes of May 1968 in Paris – during which conservative authority and conventional values were challenged – are looked upon as, in effect, Utopia's last stand; hope in the prospect of alternatives has progressively ebbed since then. Indeed, the dominance of instrumentalist, capitalist realism makes a consideration of Lefebvre's utopianism a matter of urgency (Coleman 2005, 2011; Harvey 2000; Levitas 2000, 2013; Moylan and Baccolini 2007; Sargent 2006).

In the theory and practice of architecture and city making, the tendency towards irony, autonomy and acquiescence during the past four decades has largely paralysed both. Everyday settings dominated by spectacle translate into a dwindling terrain for consciousness unencumbered by the reigning uniformity of totalising systems. Against this backdrop, the 'prodigious diversity' of 'living' that prevailed before the spread of modernity emerges as a counterproposal for Lefebvre. According to him: 'Today we see a worldwide tendency to uniformity. [. . .] For example, in the domain of architecture, a variety of local, regional and national architectural styles has given way to "architectural urbanism," a universalizing system of structures and functions in supposedly rational geometric forms' (Lefebvre 1987: 7, 8). The 'supposedly rational geometric forms' identified by Lefebvre obviously refer to orthodox modern architecture and planning. Although in the ensuing years, high-profile architecture appears to have overcome to some extent the pervasive 'universalizing system of structures and functions' that Lefebvre writes about, the dominance of icon buildings and standardised building technologies and assemblies has only made this condition more widespread.

More than ever, the built environment is characterised by the 'non-places' that French anthropologist Marc Augé attributes to the condition he has dubbed 'supermodernity' (Augé 1995). In this regard, the most universal function and structure is the shopping mall; a fully optimised setting of capitalist consumption, only surpassed by the Internet. From hospital to airport and from school to library, and especially city centres, the logic of the shopping mall dominates, threatening to erase territorial and functional distinctiveness. Outlets of national and multinational chain stores – Costa Coffee and Starbucks, for example – have become a common feature of hospitals and schools, to say nothing of airports and motorway service stations. Our willing naturalisation of the shopping mall as the key setting of daily life highlights how the everyday may be simultaneously a site of resistance to universalising sameness, and also ripe for critique, of the sort that Utopia makes possible. As Lefebvre observed, it 'constitutes the platform upon which the bureaucratic society of controlled consumerism is erected' (Lefebvre 1987: 9). And yet it is the very collusion of the everyday with the abstract and impersonal forces that increasingly dominate it that suggests just how those forces may be overcome in a utopian moment that reveals alternatives to space and life alike. Admittedly this claim can seem little more than an impossibly clever paradox, but for Lefebvre, it is the very pervasiveness and apparent banality of the everyday that permits it to harbour such a possibility. As he observed, the everyday 'is [. . .] the most universal and most unique condition, the most social and the most individuated, the most obvious and the most hidden', which also makes it the 'sole surviving common sense referent and point of reference' (Lefebvre 1987: 9). The everyday holds out the promise of an in-depth understanding of the present while also being the source of its radical re-invention, which places it at the heart of Lefebvre's utopianism:

> **The concept of everydayness does not therefore designate a system, but rather a denominator common to existing systems. [. . .] Banality? Why should the study of the banal itself be banal? Are not the surreal, the extraordinary, the surprising, even the magical, also part of the real? Why wouldn't the concept of everydayness reveal the extraordinary in the ordinary?**
>
> **(Lefebvre 1987: 9)**

The 'extraordinary' revealed in the ordinariness of the everyday constitutes its most resistant, even radical, moment. Real transformation could even emerge out of such a moment. But identifying promising moments in the midst of the everyday and tapping into their potential requires concentrated effort: 'Modernity and everydayness constitute a deep structure that a critical analysis can work to uncover' (Lefebvre 1987: 11). Getting at how modernity and the everyday form a web of oscillating super and substructure (the forms of state and social consciousness in a society – superstructure – that are determined by the economic relations of production in that society – substructure, and vice versa) promises to illuminate those 'certain conditions' required for 'transforming the everyday' (Lefebvre 1987: 11). But Lefebvre is adamant that 'to change life, society, space, architecture, even the city must change' (Lefebvre 1987: 11).

Lefebvre's assertion that 'space, architecture' and 'the city' must change for life and society to change is a radical challenge to the purging of Utopia and social purpose that was a by-product of the attacks on orthodox modern architecture and city planning which began in the 1950s. As such, it is also diametrically opposed to the shift away from apparent *idealism* towards so-called *reality* developing since the 1960s. The belief (justified or not) that Utopia, or a social purpose for architecture, are untenable has taken two primary forms since the 1970s: eclectic and sardonic historical allusion on the one hand, and the *autonomy project* of architecture on the other, by which the tasks of architecture are limited to primarily formal or typological concerns in response to architects' diminished authority and reduced influence within the building industry of capitalist production (nevertheless, both are aligned with the 'theory explosion' of the same period) (Coleman 2005: 63–87; Hays 1998, 2000, 2010; Somol 1997). However, once done with Utopia, architecture and urbanism lost a significant source of direction, and they seem to have become increasingly irrelevant. The void has largely been filled by the limited perspectives of real estate development and media, as well as by the logic of the art market and fashion. The dominant characteristic of architectural production and regeneration of the city in our time is a comingling of spectacle and positivist reductionism – a sort of capitalist realism – presented as though it were the only possibility. In a sense, the first moment of a renewed utopianism for architecture begins with a recollected conviction that changing 'space, architecture' and 'the city' establishes a *counterform* to also changing life and society. It is hard to imagine a more devastating critique of the prevailing modes of architectural or urban practices, or one more fundamentally utopian.

Lefebvre's assertion that 'space, architecture' and 'the city' must change for life and society to change is a radical challenge to the purging of Utopia and social purpose that was a by-product of the attacks on orthodox modern architecture and city planning.

Because Lefebvre's ideas on practice and the methods he elaborated for thinking the apparently unthinkable are fundamentally utopian, it would be impossible not to embrace the social potential of Utopia he theorised, and the counter-practices it suggests when working with his ideas in researching (and inventing) architecture and the city. Indeed, by reaffirming the enduring value of Utopia in imagining significant alternatives, Lefebvre's writing is as much a consideration of Utopia as it is utopian as well. By revealing Utopia as much more than some defunct historical oddity, Lefebvre exposes its exile from architecture as little more than an affirmation of social and political emptiness:

> Today more than ever there is no theory without utopia. Otherwise a person is content to record what he sees before his eyes; he doesn't go too far – he keeps his eyes fixed on so called reality: he is a *realist* . . . but he doesn't think! There is no theory that neither explores a possibility nor tries to discover an orientation.
>
> (Lefebvre 2009 [1970]: 178)

In demonstrating how theory is a product of Utopia, especially for making possible escape beyond the limiting perspectives of so-called reality, Lefebvre re-introduces the necessary link between imagining possibilities and productive thought. According to him, demanding the impossible is a first step towards other possibilities, and a fundamentally theoretical orientation, unthinkable without Utopia.

Lefebvre's other vision of Utopia

Conceivably, the limited influence of Lefebvre's thinking on actual design practices is a product of his utopianism, his stalwart Marxism and perhaps even his extensions of Marx's thought (Lefebvre 1968b). The notable failures of modern architecture, ostensibly associated with Utopia, surely have something to do with this, but Lefebvre shows that the disappointments and failures of the modern city do not lie with Utopia or with incompetence but rather with the limitations anti-utopianism places upon augmented social and physical reality (Coleman, A. 1985; Rowe and Koetter 1978). Ultimately, the sway of neoliberalism on social life and the built environment far outstrips the influence any putatively autonomous architect or urban designer could ever have.

Lefebvre's model of supple utopian-Marxism, open to dreams and imagination of the sort Utopia makes possible, enabled his move beyond an uncompromisingly radical position in which improbable revolution is thought to be the only way to achieve social transformation. Equally, in response to the rigidities of state socialism, Lefebvre was committed to positive engagement with the present, particularly with what he saw as the always-present potential for recapturing the meaning and value of everyday life in its depth from the seductive nothingness of spectacle; possible because some crack can always be found, even in apparently totally closed systems. However, he believed that making the most of such cracks requires an inherently utopian vision of possibility for reimagining and revaluing social life and the city as its setting. In Lefebvre's view, only the most specialised activities could be truly free of Utopia, while the insipid thought inherent in such specialisation assures dreary results (in the form of fragmented cities and diminished social life):

> **Who is not a utopian today? Only narrowly specialized practitioners working to order without the slightest critical examination of stipulated norms and constraints, only those not very interesting people escape utopianism.**
>
> **(Lefebvre 1996 [1968a]: 151)**

The virtue of embracing Utopia as a way to overcome positivism is that it begins to make the previously impossible seem increasingly possible, though the narrow specialisation which often characterises professionalised thought and behaviour tends to exclude such a perspective.

> Of course, as soon as one eschews the overpowering philosophy of positivism (which is nothing more than the absences of thought), it becomes rather difficult to distinguish between the possible and the impossible. Nevertheless, there is today, especially in the domain that concerns us, no theory without utopia. The architects, like the urban planners, know this perfectly well.
>
> (Lefebvre 2009 [1970]: 178–179)

The fragmentation of the modern city is analogised in the range of separations capitalism demands, including specialisation, and the isolation of art from life, theory from practice, and work from play, which have come to characterise social and cultural life during the past century or so. The division of labour is the most significant separation formulated by capitalism and leads to all the others that follow, which also have a profound influence on the organisation of the modern city (zoning for example). In contradistinction, Utopia is comprehensive, entailing conceptions of a whole in which social life can be imagined as reunified.

To achieve its aims, capitalism must be ruthlessly pragmatic, resulting in dramatically unequal societies and spatial practices that uncannily express it. In its own way, applied Marxism has been equally pragmatic, even if only apparently so. It presupposes centralisation as a means of organising production, which inevitably encourages bloated bureaucracy and party functionaries who attempt to manage society unimaginatively (producing a concomitant spatiality). In its criticism of existing conditions, Utopia articulates an alternative to bureaucracy and its spatiality. Because reality is never complete, (re)invention of alternatives remains a constant possibility. Lefebvre necessarily begins with Marx's sustained critique of capitalism in order to deal with its propensity for dissolving integrated social life, but he does not stop there.

> Marxian thought alone is not sufficient, but it is indispensable for understanding the present-day world. In our view, it is the starting point for any such understanding, though its basic concepts have to be elaborated, refined, and complemented by other concepts where necessary. It is part of

> the modern world, an original, fruitful, and irreplaceable element in our present-day situation, with particular relevance to one specialized science – sociology.
>
> (Lefebvre 1968b: 188)

The most serious limitation of Marx and Marxism, according to Lefebvre, is the blind eye both turn towards cities which inevitably neglects the city as a crucial setting of human desire. Associated with this is Marxism's tendency to shy away from wonder, which prompted Lefebvre to theorise a sociology inspired by a critical study of Marx but unafraid to 'address itself to the relations between the following concepts, which are still insufficiently distinguished: ideology and knowledge, Utopia and anticipation of the future, poetry and myth' (Lefebvre 1968b: 87–88). Locating a place within Marxian thought for wishes, dreams, poetry and Utopia certainly ranks amongst Lefebvre's most significant achievements. His nuanced approach to Marx is analogous to his optimistic belief that it is possible to transform the present by critically engaging with it. Reform of this sort, organised according to the logic of Utopia as a way of imagining alternative social and spatial arrangements, is something of an applied Utopia, but characterised by an open-endedness that resists the sort of inflexible closure that so often transforms utopian experiments from hope to despair. Accordingly, Lefebvre could envision superior alternatives achievable step by step that benefit from opportunities for rethinking consequences along the way. Importantly, Lefebvre's utopian practice was not so totalising as to be trounced by time and necessity. The real benefit of this reworking of Utopia is that it demonstrates how an augmented existence is ever recoverable from the remnants of brighter moments that hint at the reconstitution of social life and the city as its setting. Collapsing the divide 'between the possible and the impossible', even incrementally, promises to make transformation appear achievable simply by bringing it slightly closer. Clearly, Lefebvre's romantic vision of recuperation is fundamentally utopian. In the traces of alternatives persisting in memory, and in what remains of the pre-capitalist city, Lefebvre believed individuals really could gain access to a more authentic, directly lived, everyday life. When awareness of this potential touches consciousness, even gently, we may begin to desire reform and realise it together, by way of Utopia (which is why the disaggregating instability of constant redevelopment and incessant organisational change are key features of the modern capitalist city and upended social life alike).

Clearly, Lefebvre's romantic vision of recuperation is fundamentally utopian. In the traces of alternatives persisting in memory, and in what remains of the pre-capitalist city, Lefebvre believed individuals really could gain access to a more authentic, directly lived, everyday life.

Ultimately, for Lefebvre, Utopia is central to imagining the *possible impossible* of places constructible in the present, where general and biographical moments can be recollected. Urgent as such a prospect might be, Lefebvre was not so impatient as to believe that utopian revolutionary efforts must be fully implemented as material reality all at once. In fact, by relinquishing the determinist mind-set of positivism he cleared a space for thought, which, with its reflective propensity, assures that action would not be an end in itself. In this way, Utopia's vocation is imagining the real *possibility* of what seems *impossible* only in this moment.

Dialectical utopianism

Like the nineteenth-century utopian socialists who preceded him, Lefebvre acknowledges the centrality of direct action and practice for the realisation of an alternative; the theoretical elegance of abstract exercises is not enough. Despite the limited application of his ideas in practice, and the scant opportunities for testing them in real projects, Lefebvre's conceptualisations of a vital urban milieu, liberated from capitalism, still harbour great potential for cities.

For Lefebvre, research is key to a utopianism that is constitutive rather than pathological (that is, a Utopia that is partial, constructive and gradual, as opposed to totalising, destructive and hasty). The conception of Utopia as also having a positive side is related to Lefebvre's understanding that there is a dialectical relationship between the possible and the impossible: 'Nowadays dreams, imagination and utopianism are exploring the dialectic between the possible and the impossible' (Lefebvre 1995 [1962]: 357). Subjecting projects to dialectical analysis offers a way to test their possible outcomes at an early stage. A dialectical consideration of a desirable *Not Yet* promises a means for, as Lefebvre puts it, 'superseding' both 'classicism and romanticism'. Equally, the defamiliarising capacities of Romanticism make it worth holding onto as well. Lefebvre develops his idea of a dialectal utopianism in what follows:

> **Only a reasoned but dialectical use of utopianism will permit us to illuminate the present in the name of the future, to criticize what has been accomplished, to criticize bourgeois or socialist everyday life. [. . .] Only this dialectical use of utopianism as a method will allow us to *programme* our thought and our lives, and to retain a critical consciousness amid all this mixture of overblown aestheticism, art in decline, ideologism, [. . .] it is no longer a question of one leap into the distant future over the head of the present and the near future, but of exploring the possible using the present as a starting point.**
>
> **(Lefebvre 1995 [1962]: 357)**

Key in the preceding quote is Lefebvre's assertion that 'dialectical utopianism' can open up possibilities for the future by way of critical engagement with the present. This contribution to Utopia as method is significant because it charts how the possible can be given a concrete form even before realisation, at least within consciousness. Importantly, ideas of the future that emerge out of a critique of what already exists, along with the incremental exploration of their potential in relation to the reality of present conditions, lessens the danger of the possible-impossible of these ideas deforming into absolutist (pathological) abstractions of the (constitutive) utopian visions they house; a positive development only conceivable because,

> the possible and the utopian method can no longer be synonymous with foresight, prophecy, adventurism or the vague consciousness of the future. We can no longer see utopianism as an abstract principle like hope, projection, willpower or goodwill, 'prescience', 'values', or axiology [theory of moral values].

> (Lefebvre 1995 [1962]: 357)

Liberated from what Lefebvre asserts are outmoded and restrictive conceptualisations of its capacities, utopianism – of a dialectical concrete sort based in everyday life and a critical engagement with it – could be put to work confronting the crucial problems of new towns (Lefebvre 1995 [1962]: 357). As the stage upon which life plays out, the built environment presents itself as the most compelling ground for deploying dialectical utopianism to test the limits and possibilities (the relative *possible* of the apparently *impossible*) of achievable alternatives.

Experimental and theoretical Utopias

In its 'old fashioned sense', Utopia is problematic for Lefebvre, largely because of its absolutist tendency, and for its propensity to deceive with impossible promises of fulfilment at the scales of individual and society alike. However, Lefebvre argues that what he calls 'transduction' provides a method – intellectual and practical – for reforming Utopia by working out and constructing possible objects 'from information related to reality and a problematic posed by this reality'. Thus, transduction balances its operations between 'the conceptual framework used' to identify problems and invent responses, and 'empirical observations' of reality, which acts as a bulwark against the dissociative abstraction associated with capitalist reduction and the alienation it fosters. By providing a crucial feedback loop within utopian thinking, transduction 'introduces rigour in invention and knowledge in utopia', and thereby releases its potential for radical transformation (that is concrete and achievable) (Lefebvre 1996 [1968a]: 141).

Transduction. This is an intellectual operation which can be methodically carried out and which differs from classical induction, deduction and the construction of 'models', simulation as well as the simple statement of hypothesis. Transduction elaborates and constructs a theoretical object, a possible object from information related to reality and a problematic posed by this reality. Transduction assumes an incessant feed back between the conceptual framework used and empirical observations. Its theory (methodology), gives shape to certain spontaneous operations of the planner, the architect, the sociologist, the politician and the philosopher. It introduces rigour in invention and knowledge in utopia.

(Lefebvre 1996 [1968a]: 151)

As defined by Lefebvre, 'transduction' works upon information drawn from existing reality to construct 'a possible object' that in turn becomes an object of inquiry for elaborating on the very possibility it represents. Although this possible object is theoretical, or conceptual, inasmuch as it does not yet exist, it is squarely rooted in the real, from which it emerges. With its origins in reality, transduction benefits from a continuous feedback loop between a possibility that exceeds that reality, and the real as a basis for testing its potential to actually do so. Of particular interest in the context of this book is Lefebvre's conviction that transduction is analogous to the inventive practices of architects.

As defined by Lefebvre, 'transduction' works upon information drawn from existing reality to construct 'a possible object' that in turn becomes an object of inquiry for elaborating on the very possibility it represents.

Transduction represents a significant step forward in utopian thinking: making possible a truly experimental Utopia, entailing the testing of, elaborating on and correcting of utopian propositions from the start. Utopianism of this sort benefits from an experimental method for generating and testing alternatives, enabling them to surpass the present while being grounded in it nonetheless. Transduction makes it possible to overcome the harsh constraints of narrow specialisation of more familiar varieties of positivist (pathological) utopias. The most significant value of transduction for Utopia is to make explicit its experimental propensity while introducing a systematic method for testing its propositions.

> *Experimental utopia.* [. . .] All are utopians, including those futurists and planners who project Paris in the year 2,000 and those engineers who made Brasilia! But there are several utopianisms. Would not the worst be that utopianism which does not utter its name, [and] covers itself with positivism [. . .]?
>
> (Lefebvre 1996 [1968a]: 151)

Only when 'utopia is tempered by very concrete analyses' and tested can the alternatives it proposes be responsive to the concrete conditions of the everyday, which in turn prevents it from becoming abstract (Lefebvre 1996 [1968a]: 97). Equally, 'Utopia controlled by dialectical reason serves as a safeguard against supposedly scientific fictions and visions gone astray' (Lefebvre 1996 [1968a]: 156). All of which emphasises the importance of experimentation for Utopia:

> Utopia is to be considered experimentally by studying its implications and consequences on the ground. These can surprise. What are and would be the most successful places? How can they be discovered? According to which criteria? What are the times and rhythms of daily life which are inscribed and prescribed in these 'successful' spaces favourable to happiness? That is interesting.
>
> (Lefebvre 1996 [1968a]: 151)

It might seem self-evident that any planning and architecture project could be greatly improved by 'studying its implications and consequences on the ground', but in common practice this rarely occurs; at least in part because operating in this way is of little interest, because the surprises such experimentation might reveal would challenge professional confidence in the outcomes of projects. As interesting a problem as this professional insecurity is, Lefebvre focuses on other reasons why experimentation is resisted, which he believe derive from the propensity of architects to elaborate their 'dogmatized [. . .] ensemble of significations [. . .] not from the significations perceived and lived by those who inhabit, but from their interpretation of inhabiting. It is graphic and visual, tending towards metalanguage. [. . .] [T]heir system tends to close itself off, impose itself and elude all criticism' (Lefebvre 1996 [1968a]: 152). Because architects' very operations constitute an abstract system of ocularcentric symbols that privilege appearance and vision over experience by the other senses, testing on the ground can seem irrelevant. Questions regarding 'most successful places' and 'the times and rhythms of daily life [. . .] inscribed and prescribed in "successful" spaces favourable to happiness' remain largely unasked by architects because they are fundamentally bodily, rather than visual. Even in those instances when such questions may be of interest, a graphic and visual understanding and representation of reality usually overwhelms them. However, like Utopia, architecture could become simultaneously both more open and grounded if its practices were informed by an 'analysis of the real (an analysis which is never exhaustive or without residue)', suggested by the methods of transduction.

Lefebvre's recuperation of the radical potential of Utopia makes the possible-impossible more conceivable. Even so, the 'the distant possible' of this Utopia continues to distinguish it from the prognosticating Utopia of futurists and planners (Lefebvre 2003 [1961b]: 86). He inverts convention, inasmuch as his Utopia is not 'an abstract ideal', or a deception 'in which fiction and reality are thoroughly mixed', and 'signs' rather than 'things' dominate. Typically, Utopia is characterised as an abstraction that is at best 'half real and half imaginary', offering little in the way of opening up horizons on the possible (Lefebvre 2003 [1966/2001]: 132–133):

> **Utopia attaches itself to numerous more or less distant and unknown or misunderstood realities, but no longer to real and daily life. It is no longer begotten in the absences and lacunae [the gaps] which cruelly puncture surrounding reality. The gaze turns away, leaves the horizon, loses itself in the clouds, elsewhere.**
>
> **(Lefebvre 1996 [1968a]: 163)**

This passage clarifies Lefebvre's opposing senses of Utopia. Utopia loses its edge as it becomes more abstract. It: 'loses itself in the clouds' as it 'attaches itself to [. . .] distant and unknown or misunderstood realities'. In contradistinction, concrete utopia 'attaches itself [. . .] to real and daily life' and springs from 'the absences and lacunae which cruelly puncture surrounding reality'. Thought of in this way, 'Utopia, i.e., a theory of the distantly possible, is not an "eschatology", a theory that the process of becoming might be brought to an end. It is the very concrete and positive idea of a history which has at last been oriented, directed and mastered by knowledge and willpower' (Lefebvre 2008 [1961a]: 73). Setting aside fantasies of eschatological finality, in the way Lefebvre does, frees Utopia to orientate thought and action towards identifying what is missing and filling gaps. It is, however, an open process with no certain conclusion, which is why Utopia's capacity for reorientation and expanding awareness is so valuable.

For Lefebvre, the 'possible-impossible' and 'utopia' (in the positive) are interchangeable: 'Exploration of the possible-impossible has another name: U-topia' (Lefebvre 2003 [1970/2001]: 185). (The separation of 'U' from 'topia' here respects Sir Thomas More's [1478–1535] paradoxical coinage of 'Utopia' which derives from the Greek '*eu*' [good] and '*ou*' [no], plus 'topia' [*topos*, place], and suggests Utopia as a 'good non place', or, as Lefebvre puts it, a 'possible-impossible'.) According to him, concrete Utopia 'alone enables us to think and act'; he goes so far as to assert that 'now more than ever there is no thought without u-topia, in other words, without an exploration of the possible and the impossible, i.e. the possible-impossible conceived dialectically' (Lefebvre 2003 [1970/2001]: 184). He writes:

> In a more profoundly dialectical way, the possible-impossible [Utopia] arises and shows itself in the heart of the possible [the Everyday]. And conversely, of course. There is no communication that does not include in its possibility the project of the impossible: to say everything. There is no love that does not presuppose absolute love. No knowledge that does not posit absolute knowledge, the inconceivable, unlimited and finite.
>
> (Lefebvre 2003 [1970/2001]: 186)

Alternatives can arise out of the everyday precisely because it is formed by the habitual, the individually and collectively well-known, ordinary activities of individuals and communities. The everyday is also 'elusory' and as such 'evinces a not insignificant degree of resistance' to the 'panoptic sweep of bureaucratic surveillance, indexing and control', which struggles to register the 'local knowledges and practices of the quotidian, mundane, habitual that characterize the greater reality of daily life' (Gardiner 2004: 229).

Modern architecture and planning have been conventionally diagnosed as utopian. In reality, in almost every instance, they are anything but utopian. To this day, most city modernisation is the product of impulse (and so-called market forces) rather than careful thought, which deprives projects – utopian or otherwise – of the benefits to be gained from measured reflection on the potential consequences of any plan. Realisation usually takes shape with little regard for those most affected by plans, even as the idealisation that motivated them is presented as inevitable, as a product of rational thought. Opening up a gap between projection and realisation could counteract the hazards of realisation. When reflection is relinquished, the drift is inexorably towards absolutism. Unsurprisingly, then, most urban redevelopment practices are, as Lefebvre observed, actually positivism masquerading as Utopia.

Architects and urban planners often make wild claims for their work, yet thoughtful reflection and research is a crucially absent practical dimension of many redevelopment schemes, in existing cities and instantaneous new ones alike. Although the potential liveability of cities or buildings are often represented as quantitative or artistic certainties, built results inevitably disappoint when projects do not respond to the qualitative dimensions of life, or its specific everyday habits.

The methods proposed by Lefebvre, informed by Utopia and Romanticism and organised according to 'transduction' could direct architectural and urban research towards questions about those qualities that most affect people in the

'Designed to be Empty?', Waterloo Square, Newcastle upon Tyne, UK

specific social and spatial contexts in which they live. Asking such questions might seem an unnecessary diversion at cross-purposes to the production of seductive images and professional mythologies, but that would be to miss the value that Lefebvre ascribes to the underexplored practical side of Utopia.

Lefebvre's identification of Utopia's underexplored theoretical and experimental dimension aligns with his ultimate interest in alternative spatial practices. Equally, by emphasising Utopia's propensity for research, Lefebvre shows how it can be central to theorising social, political and spatial alternatives. Utopia as an opening-up of prospects onto 'profound economic and socio-political modifications', as well as spatial ones, even if never fully achieved, in no way negates its value for reimagining habitual practices (Lefebvre 2009 [1976]: 176). As complete realisation is impossible, no project will ever become fully actualised. Nevertheless, too little consideration is given to the provisional nature of (economic, city and architectural) plans.

Lefebvre's identification of Utopia's underexplored theoretical and experimental dimension aligns with his ultimate interest in alternative spatial practices. Equally, by emphasising Utopia's propensity for research, Lefebvre shows how it can be central to theorising social, political and spatial alternatives.

The Utopian prospect of Lefebvre

Lefebvre's conviction was that Utopia – a recuperated social life – could be re-drawn from cracks in the present, as an imaginative reconstitution of society. Bearing this in mind, thinking with Lefebvre entails thinking with and about Utopia. And engaging the utopian strand of Lefebvre's thinking makes contact with the most enduring aspect of his project of possibility for cities and people:

> 'Utopist!'
>
> 'And why not? For me this term has no pejorative connotations. Since I do not ratify compulsion, norms, rules and regulations; since I put all the emphasis on adaptation; since I refute "reality", and since for me what is possible is already partly real, I am indeed a utopian; you will observe that I do not say utopist; but utopian yes, a partisan of possibilities.'
>
> (Lefebvre 1984 [1971]: 192)

Architects, planners and urban designers may be profoundly discomfited by Utopia, however, Lefebvre demonstrates just how improbable reimagining the world – unbound from the enervating constraints of the given – would be without it.

To draw a positive Utopia from the everyday, 'one must', according to Lefebvre, 'want the impossible to realize the possible'. He characterised this as '*Urgent utopia*', defining it as 'a style of thinking turned toward the possible in all areas' (Lefebvre 2009 [1978]: 288). Lefebvre's accurate documentation of the conditions that affect the social life and form of present-day cities is a first step in countering the continuing concretisation of alienation in the built environment. What could be more utopian, or more urgent?

CHAPTER 3

The production of space

To speak of 'producing space' sounds bizarre, so great is the sway still held by the idea that empty space is prior to whatever ends up filling it. Questions immediately arise here: what spaces? And what does it mean to speak of 'producing space'?

(Lefebvre 1991 [1974]: 15)

The aim of this book is to detonate this state of affairs. More specifically it aims to foster confrontation between those ideas and propositions which illuminate the modern world even if they do not govern it, treating them not as isolated hypotheses, as 'thoughts' to be put under the microscope, but rather as prefigurations lying at the threshold of modernity.

(Lefebvre 1991 [1974]: 24)

The strategic hypothesis [of this work] based on space [. . .] sets itself up in clear opposition to the homogenizing efforts of the state, of political power, of the world market, and of the commodity world-tendencies [. . .] which find their practical expression through and in abstract space.

(Lefebvre 1991 [1974]: 64–65)

What we have been considering, then, is an extension [. . .] which embraces the radical critique of philosophy without, however, abandoning [. . .] the concrete universal and the import of the concept. We are concerned, in other words, with theory beyond system-building.

(Lefebvre 1991 [1974]: 399)

Problematic of *The Production of Space*

Any attempt to present an overview of Lefebvre's *The Production of Space* (1991 [1974]) must inevitably be exclusive rather than inclusive. Indeed, the depth and breadth of the book presents a particular challenge. Between the extremes of exhaustiveness and superficiality, I have attempted to render as faithfully as possible the *atmosphere* of Lefebvre's thinking, in an effort to convey the gist of *The Production of Space* without reducing it to little more than an advert for the book.

If successful, this extended presentation of the gist of *The Production of Space* will communicate something of the breathtaking range of Lefebvre's thinking, while revealing its significant interest and genuine value for architects, and anyone else with an interest in the human world we inhabit, either as a maker or contributor to it (in whatever capacity), or as a concerned person with a stake in the shape it takes. The guiding principle in my attempt to render the atmosphere of Lefebvre's thinking in *The Production of Space* has been to focus on those aspects of it with the most direct relevance for architects, students, practitioners and academics alike. The main topics that will be referred to either explicitly, or more implicitly, in the ensuing discussion are drawn directly from the myriad topics Lefebvre himself introduces in the book, including: 'Spatial Praxis', 'Representations of Space' and 'Spaces of Representation'. In addition to these three key topics, Lefebvre's consideration of 'Social Space' is central to his project in *The Production of Space* in particular, and throughout his work on the urban and everyday life more generally.

Also considered are the shades of difference between what Lefebvre calls 'works' (unique, akin to fine art) and what he identifies as 'products' (akin to a reproducible commodity), the significance of which for architecture cannot be overestimated. Equally important to an understanding of Lefebvre's project is his conviction that in modernity, 'time' has been dissociated from 'space', resulting in the dominance of 'space' to the near exclusion of 'time', except in its mechanised, clockwork, manifestation, in which rituals and festivals are replaced by the organisation of work according to the time clock (a topic returned to in the next chapter). Finally, and inextricably bound to the key themes of *The Production of Space* already introduced, 'Absolute Space'; 'Historical' or 'Relative Space'; 'Abstract Space'; and 'Contradictory Space' are also considered. Lefebvre's project for an analysis of the 'production of space' seeks nothing less than to develop an understanding of how capitalism and state controls are 'spatialized', but also to reveal how the 'abstract space' of capitalist production can be resisted by the remnants of 'absolute space' that survive in the habits of 'everyday life'.

In an attempt to draw out the overarching theme of *The Production of Space*, it is worth beginning with Lefebvre's clarification of the utopian project at its core, which he articulates near the book's conclusion as 'the project of a different society':

> This book has been informed from beginning to end by a *project*, though this may at times have been discernible only by reading between the lines. I refer to the project of a different society, a different mode of production, where social practice would be governed by different conceptual determinations.
>
> **(419)**

Undeniably, Lefebvre can present a challenge to even the most sympathetic reader; the complexity and range of his writing can on occasion defy attempts to render it coherent, which is why it makes good sense to introduce Lefebvre's own declaration of his intentions at the beginning of this discussion of the far-reaching and quite long *Production of Space*. And yet, doing so is not fully in keeping with Lefebvre's project, the aims of which he readily acknowledges are hidden 'between the lines'. Not only does he shed light on why he has proceeded in this way, he also implies why attempting to introduce the sort of clarification he arrives at only at the end of the book should remain there, rather than being placed up front (as I have heretically done here):

> No doubt this project could be explicitly formulated; to do so would involve heightening the distinctions between 'project', 'plan' and 'programme', or between 'model' and 'way forward'. But it is far from certain that such an approach would allow us to make forecasts or to generate what are referred to as 'concrete' proposals. The project would still remain an abstract one. Though opposed to the abstraction of the

dominant space, it would not transcend that space. Why? Because the road of the 'concrete' leads via active theoretical and practical negation, via counter-projects or counter-plans. And hence via an active and massive intervention on the part of the 'interested parties'.

(419)

The crucial point here is that understanding must precede action if any endeavour is to actually have a chance of transcending the sorts of spaces Lefebvre subjects to a sustained criticism throughout *The Production of Space*. Only by working through the book, by following all of its diversions, and through processing all of its insights, can one develop a more substantial understanding of the production of space (419). With this in mind, much as I have tried to do justice to the book and to the intensity of Lefebvre's thought more generally, my attempt is no substitute for wrestling with the primary source, which it is hoped interested readers will want to do on the basis of the present discussion.

The crucial point here is that understanding must precede action if any endeavour is to actually have a chance of transcending the sorts of spaces Lefebvre subjects to a sustained criticism throughout *The Production of Space*.

From space to place

In his effort to understand the 'production of space' – by which what is really at stake are 'places' – Lefebvre returns again and again to the wide gap that separates the products of professionals, such as those of architects and planners, from their intended inhabitants – citizens, individuals – and the unfolding of everyday life. The alienation of individuals from the built environment they inhabit leads to 'disillusion', which 'leaves space empty – an emptiness that words convey' (97). Even if it can seem as though people have become more interested in architecture during the past twenty to thirty years than at any other time in living memory, the consumption of architecture as object dominates. Architecture is primarily appreciated and evaluated by way of vision alone, as though it were located in the distance or as an image, akin to either a thing in a gallery, or on a screen, or in an advertisement, rather than 'the setting in which we live' (92). Overall, the contemporary built environment is characterised by 'spaces' that 'are strange: homogeneous, rationalized, and as such constraining; yet at the same time utterly dislocated' (97). It is characterised by the loss of 'formal boundaries [. . .] between town and country, between centre and periphery, between suburbs and city centres, between the domain of automobiles and the domain of people' (97). Far from the contemporary built environment being just as we want it, the reward of alienation it offers is less some kind of liberating homogeneity and anonymity, than, as Lefebvre sees it, a paradoxical situation made up of the dissolution of formal boundaries 'between happiness and unhappiness', and the rigid separations, found in ' "public facilities", blocks of flats, "environments for living" ' that are 'separated' and 'assigned in isolated fashion to unconnected "sites" ', in 'spaces' which are 'themselves [. . .] specialized just as operations are in the social and technical division of labour' (97–98).

While many architects attempt to make a virtue of conditions of division and isolation, the alienation that arises from this as a by-product of capitalism and the organisation of the state and commerce more generally, is set apart from consciousness as a matter of necessity, or convenience. Finding a purpose for architecture when it is subsumed by the building industry as a small part of it – as 'excess value', urban adornment or 'icon' – is exceedingly difficult. Although buildings as 'objects' on isolated building plots might seem to liberate each individual work of architecture and its architect to the significant pleasures of his or her own apparent creativity, this barely veils the complicity of such buildings in the fragmentation of the urban environment, including widespread disregard for the everyday life encroached upon and threatened with dissolution. Equally, this approach transforms buildings into commodities – products.

In *The Production of Space*, Lefebvre calls attention to the problems of 'representations' –the degree to which images of things offer at best a partial view, and at worst promise to conceal and deceive. Although architects cannot escape representations, Lefebvre's doubts about the efficacy of images in making the world knowable could at least encourage them to focus on this problem as worthy of reflection, both with regard to the significant translations that inevitably take place in the move from drawings (and other architectural images) to buildings, while alerting architecture students and practitioners to the seductive deceptions of the images they create, which tend to prematurely convince them of the value of their own work. Concentration on the problematic of visual representation could also direct attention to the gaps that reliance on such 'information' establishes between apparent expertise and daily life, or actual lived experience, which can never be anticipated (or captured) in a drawing or any other representations. In this regard, Lefebvre goes so far as to argue that 'the image kills' (97).

'City as Commodity: Computer Simulation of the *Future*?', computer image of building under construction, Newcastle upon Tyne, UK

Overcoming Cartesian logic

Foremost amongst Lefebvre's objectives in *The Production of Space* is to mount a challenge to the idea of 'geometrical space' and the idea of space as 'an empty area'. Lefebvre attributes the rise to the dominance of a view of space as empty to Descartes and the absolutist tendencies of 'Cartesian logic' (1). The limitation of these views of space is that 'the concept of space' they promote is primarily 'a mathematical one', which inevitably makes a consideration of 'social space' seem 'strange' (1). In the realm of architecture, the idea of space as geometrical or mathematical and thus empty prevails, encouraging a predominant idea of architecture as an autonomous object in space, positioned for aesthetic appreciation. Although an understanding of architecture and the city as social concerns might exist, an abstract and mathematical detachment overshadows the key task of city making as the production of social space.

Associated with his challenge to the idea of space as empty, Lefebvre argues that the fundamentally abstract nature of mathematical theories severs the ties between an empirical grasp of nature – of the real world – largely by demoting the value of the senses in relation to developing understandings of the world and phenomena. According to him, the concept of space as an empty area shifts philosophical considerations of space – such as ancient Greek philosopher Aristotle (384–322 BC) advanced – to a 'science of space', which decouples space from time, and thus also from considerations of social life as unfolding in space (2–3). Briefly stated, Lefebvre's counter-project is to define space on the basis of its specificity and to bridge 'the gap between the theoretical (epistemological) realm and the practical one, between mental and social, between the space of the philosophers and the space of people who deal with material things' (4). To achieve this, Lefebvre argues that the centrality of social life and social practices to any discussion of space must first be recuperated. His quarrel, though, was not with scientific abstractions of space alone; rather, in his view, technocrats are the real problem, with their propensity for applying just such abstractions to the social realm by way of theoretical practices. Although Lefebvre does not believe it is actually possible to separate the 'mental space' of abstraction from the 'real space' of 'lived experience', the very attempt to do so 'tends to reinforce [. . .] a banal "consensus" ' (6).

Descriptions of space or 'readings' of space are less interesting for Lefebvre than the development of a history of spatial practices in relation to prevailing modes of production at the time of their emergence and application. When considered in this way, the production of space is revealed as largely determined by prevailing modes of production and their organisation, as reflecting conceptions of mental space. For example, the dominance of separations in our time – of labour, of uses, of theory from practice, of space from time – relates to the prevalence of abstraction in conceptions of space, which architectural and urban spaces in turn analogise, the predominance of the alienating aspects of the visual being the most obvious example of this (7–8).

Although *The Production of Space* is filled with paradoxes, one of the most surprising is Lefebvre's conviction that the endless divisions and infinite separations of 'neocapitalist' space (which exhibit 'a dominant trend toward fragmentation, separation and disintegration') does not translate into 'overall control' being 'relinquished', but is rather 'a trend subordinated to a centre or to a centralized power' (9, 8). Not only is the hegemonic space of 'capitalism' and of 'the ruling class' characterised by 'fragmentation, separation and disintegration', this condition is one of the primary means by which the system and its elites are able to maintain their dominance, while also attempting to 'thoroughly' purge the 'world market' of 'contradictions' (9–10, 11). (For Lefebvre, 'hegemony' and 'hegemonic' relate to the dominance of one class, ideology and political, social or economic vision within a society over all other opposing visions. If 'neo-capitalism' is understood as 'hegemonic', space produced under its system of production will embody its values as the cultural dominant, resulting in 'hegemonic-space'. Conversely, 'non-hegemonic space' will somehow be produced outside of, or unencumbered by, the 'neocapitalist' cultural dominant.) As such, 'capital and capitalism "influence" practical matters relating to space, from the construction of buildings to the distribution of investments and the worldwide division of labour' (9–10). In this way, the apparent fragmentation masks an organised system of control made possible by separations that disintegrate social life.

Ever since the significant failures of high modernist architecture began to be acknowledged in the 1960s, the view that architecture must be politically and

60   THE PRODUCTION OF SPACE

socially neutral has become common. Nevertheless, Lefebvre is adamant that space is not neutral; rather, it is the carrier and communicator of the dominant ideologies that contribute to shaping it. In the contemporary condition space is shaped to eradicate difference and to communicate intolerance for it. Material as well can be shaped into a carrier of the dominant ideology in its social, political and economic systematisations that underpin that space. In turn, these dominant expressions contribute to shaping conceptions of *truth* that suffuse spaces (places/projects). However, Lefebvre is certain that this condition is never complete or total.

In consideration of Lefebvre's critique of spatializations of the dominant ideology – neocapitalism for example – any attempt to institutionalise his ideas by transforming them into either a pedagogy or a recipe for a certain kind of space, or to achieve some particular atmosphere of social space, must come to terms with the anomaly of this: Lefebvre's target is power – hegemony, the power relations shaping culture – and systematisation, which creates a number of difficulties for anyone attempting to realise some part of the designed environment using his ideas. In particular, to build, or to construct, is to be close to power; almost nothing can be done without it. The challenge in interpreting Lefebvre for architects, then, is to do so without ignoring his disputations with power in all its forms, that he sums up as 'the antagonism between a knowledge which serves power and a form of knowing which refuses to acknowledge power', to establish 'a critical and subversive form of knowledge' (10). Arguably, the possibility of subversiveness in architecture may be all but non-existent, but this does not totally rule it out. It is precisely the possibility of non-hegemonic space that interests Lefebvre. As he puts it, he is 'concerned with logico-epsitomological space, the space of social practice, the space occupied by sensory phenomena, including products of the imagination such as projects and projections, symbols and utopias' (12). In Lefebvre's view, atomisation of potentially unified concerns for space, for the human habitat, for urban space, for territorial spaces (regional to global), into the 'specializations' of architect, urban designer, economist and planner (amongst others), and working upwards in scale from house, to city, to territory 'would be brought to an end if a truly unitary theory [of space of the sort Lefebvre attempted] were to be developed' (12).

Lefebvre's target is power – hegemony, the power relations shaping culture – and systematisation, which creates a number of difficulties for anyone attempting to realise some part of the designed environment using his ideas.

Representations of the relations of production

According to Lefebvre, 'buildings, monuments, and works of art' are 'representations of the relations of production', set within space, which are 'brutal', in the sense of being explicit. As 'representations of the relations of production', buildings, cities and public spaces also embody a subsumption of 'power relations'. In Lefebvre's terms, *architecture* is not so much space as *space contains architecture*. The benefit of this understanding is that it resituates architecture within a broader realm, and as an aspect of wider concerns, and also as influenced by numerous forces not usually considered. Although Lefebvre is concerned with architecture and also with nature, for him, 'space' is primarily 'urban space', or the 'space of the city', and 'the production of space' is above all else the *production of social space* (33).

The everyday, spatial practices and the production of space are the key objects of analysis in *The Production of Space*, but none of them is either preconceived or planned. For Lefebvre, each emerges out of the routine practices of the society out of which it arises. Taken together, these objects of analysis constitute representations of a society that cannot, however, be represented before they are enacted. In this way, Lefebvre's method is first and foremost a mode of analysis, rather than an instrument of either resistance or transgression, though it could readily inform both, which Lefebvre clearly encourages.

Lefebvre alerts us to the gap between what he calls *representations of space*, which are abstract; and *representational space*, which is 'space as directly lived', but that more importantly, 'obey no rules of consistency or cohesiveness'. The value of concentrating on this gap emerges if practitioners – architects, urban designers and planners and so forth – recognise right from the start that the spaces they represent – from individual buildings and spaces to cities – are not even approximations of eventual lived reality, but rather are at best fantasies about its potential. Understood in this way, architects and so forth might well want to pay closer attention to how individuals and groups actually appropriate spaces.

Recuperating the social

Whenever architecture is discussed in terms of style, or the personal genius or artistic abilities of the architect, the discussion has already left the realm of the social and entered into that of the abstract. This mode of discourse on architecture empties it while simultaneously bringing it within the ambit of capitalist production, as both excess value and commodity fetish. In short, discussions of style reproduce a neoliberal emphasis on vacuity, on saying nothing, and meaning less. In conventional architectural discourse, buildings are considered in isolation from both the larger spatial and social realm, and from real bodies of flesh and blood. Architecture conceived (imagined as an abstraction) and perceived (observed, in a visual sense) as an object in the distance, or as autonomous, necessarily disregards both the social and the productive (directly lived, or experienced) realms. On the one hand, social life – the way buildings are suited to the lived experiences of individuals and groups – is ignored or disavowed, and on the other, buildings as the production (or reproduction) of prevailing modes of production is rarely if ever considered. Understanding architecture and urbanism according to the criteria of objects in an 'art' market (as 'useless', or without a 'function', apart from as an investment) thus risks transforming architecture and urbanism from objects of *use* into items of *exchange*, which in one instant empties both of their social content, while paradoxically contributing to the degeneration of their potential status as *works* (akin to great works of art), as opposed to as *products* (in Lefebvre's terms).

Transforming modes of production necessarily gives rise to new organisations of space. In this way, it is possible to describe space as a production, largely determined by the modes of production that give rise to it and shape it. As an example, the organisation of space produced according to the logic of factory production – of the production line, specialisation and the division of labour – marks every industrial and post-industrial city, including those in which industrial production did not predominate.

According to Lefebvre, the 'problematic of space' as primarily 'the urban sphere', and 'the city and its extensions', has displaced the 'problematic of industrialization' (89). As suggested earlier, for Lefebvre, in each instance, 'the city' is the historic core of any given city; 'its extensions' are its modern quarters and suburbs, particularly those that have developed since the latter part of the nineteenth century (89). *Everyday life*, it is worth noting, for Lefebvre is not the generic good it has largely come to represent for geographers and others. As the equivalent of 'programmed consumption', 'everyday life' is the location of bureaucratic organisation. It also reveals the reach of this system in the guise of the divisions of capitalist production and in the requirements of the state. But 'everyday life' can also be a site of possible resistance to bureaucratic organisation, the divisions of capitalist production and the requirements of the state (89). In this way, everyday life has the potential for subverting social processes and spatial practices that otherwise can seem total and eternal.

Developing a 'science of space', Lefebvre's objective in *The Production of Space*, is difficult to achieve for a number of reasons, foremost of which is the prevailing tendency to either 'describe' or 'dissect' space, rather than analysing it more holistically, or in terms of production (90–91). In fact, according to Lefebvre, this propensity results in the fragmentation of spaces, both conceptually and practically, as any modern city readily confirms. The situation is perhaps not generally questioned because it is in harmony with the divisions endemic to contemporary social conditions, in particular the separations intrinsic to capitalism; for example, the mania for specialisations that characterises the current situation (even in the guise of *interdisciplinarity*). Another consequence of a divided approach to understanding space is to abstract it as an object of investigation considered as neutral, emphasising either 'objects in space' or

64   THE PRODUCTION OF SPACE

empty spaces 'without objects'. Such 'partial representations', according to Lefebvre, confound any search for a deeper understanding of space. In his view, development of a more substantial 'science of space' must inevitably 'rediscover time', in particular 'the time of production [. . .] in and through space' (91).

The implications of this for architects are significant, throwing architecture into question as a specialised discipline, somehow independent of urban planning, for example, or as autonomous from social life. Equally, Lefebvre's identification of the obstacles to a deeper understanding of space – of its (social) production – throws up the problem of zoning and the real estate market, which makes it all but impossible to develop a more integrated city, in which space and its context could form a more complex unity. Lefebvre's position also challenges the habit of thinking of buildings in isolation from their surroundings. In contradistinction, he encourages thinking of surroundings as forming the larger context (space) that individual works of architecture sit within and contribute to establishing or completing. The spaces between buildings – squares and streets – are therefore emphasised by Lefebvre, not least because they constitute so much of the social space of cities.

As an adjunct of the now conventional emphasis on the conceptualisation of individual buildings in isolation, there is the equally distorting tendency to neglect *use* in social terms beyond a limited idea of technical functionalism. Lefebvre's insights problematize both, making it difficult to persist in thinking about individual works of architecture as being either autonomous or akin to works of art set apart within galleries or museums, and thus unencumbered by social occupation. Additionally, no understanding of space, of architecture or the production and inhabitation of both is possible without a consideration of time (91). Some examples of the persistence of abstracting tendencies in architecture include the stubborn emphasis on *clients* rather than *communities*; another is that although talking about architectural *form* comes quite easily, considerations of *content* – the social and the political – are far more difficult, beyond preoccupations with strategy. Above all else, architectural discourse has become formalist, generally speaking a language of aesthetics divorced from ethics, experience and the body.

The Production of Space may be a history of space, but it is more than that. It is also a manifesto and a treatise. The book's most profoundly utopian dimension is the ever-present shadow of alternatives that lay ahead in the future, and which are informed by Lefebvre's highly developed critical-historical perspective on the nature of settlement and the way desire, as much as ideology, is embodied in gesture, as well as in the spaces that extend from them and which they define. For Lefebvre, space is understood through action or event; not the detached, abstract, and intellectual acts of decoding signs to get at an understanding of what they symbolise.

The Production of Space may be a history of space, but it is more than that. It is also a manifesto and a treatise. The book's most profoundly utopian dimension is the ever-present shadow of alternatives that lay ahead in the future.

The limited possibilities of the abstract space of current modes of production, of global capitalism, according to Lefebvre, embody 'at best a technological utopia, a sort of computer simulation for the future, or of the possible, within the framework of the real – the framework of the existing mode of production' (9). The point is that if the possible is imagined within the present form of the real, it is restricted to the significant limits of technological utopias, which are at best a form of prognostication, in which what already exists is extended towards its logical, though already imaginable conclusion. According to Lefebvre, technological utopias of this sort are 'a common feature not just of many science-fiction novels but also of all kinds of projects concerned with space, be those of architecture, urbanism or social planning' (9). Nevertheless, he does not believe that '[t]he substitution of a negative and critical utopia of space (or of "man" or society) for the dominant technological utopia is [. . .] sufficient' (25). In this view, he argues that 'critical theory [. . .] has had its day' because 'the opposition it can mount

66   THE PRODUCTION OF SPACE

is no longer sufficient to dislodge the dominant conditions' (25). I think in this Lefebvre is advancing a view in harmony with his conviction more generally that being *for* an alternative is far more promising than being *against* what already exists. Although he observes that '[t]he injunction to change life originated with [. . .] poets and philosophers, in the context of a negative utopianism, [. . .] it has recently fallen into the public (i.e. the political) domain', degenerating 'into political slogans' (59). The dominance of technological utopianism, and the subsuming of negative utopianism by lifestyle demands, leave us without even the implication of 'the creation, whether gradual or sudden, of a different spatial practice'. Instead, there 'is simply the return of an idea to an ideal state'. Lefebvre argues that this condition will prevail '[s]o long as everyday life remains in thrall to abstract space, with its very concrete constraints' (59):

> [S]o long as the only improvements to occur are technical improvements of detail (for example, the frequency and speed of transportation, or relatively better amenities); so long, in short, as the only connection between work spaces, leisure spaces and living spaces is supplied by the agencies of political power and by their mechanisms of control – so long must the project of 'changing life' remain no more than a political rallying-cry to be taken up or abandoned according to the mood of the moment.
>
> (59–60)

At present, according to Lefebvre, there is '[t]o one side the abyss of negative Utopias', which he characterises as 'the vanity of a critical theory which works only at the level of words and ideas (i.e. at the ideological level)'. On the other side are the 'highly positive technological Utopias: the realm of "prospectivism", of social engineering and programming' (60). The non-choice confronting theoretical thought – between 'negative Utopias' and 'technological Utopias' – presents itself to Lefebvre as both a key obstacle to completing his project and its aim:

> By seeking to point the way towards a different space, towards the space of a different (social) life and of a different mode of production, this project

▼

> straddles the breach between science and Utopia, reality and ideality, conceived and lived. It aspires to surmount these oppositions by exploring the dialectical relationship between 'possible' and 'impossible', and this both objectively and subjectively.
>
> (60)

Inevitably, the cultural dominant will seek to maintain a static condition of politics, economics and society, to say nothing of spatial practices. The limitations that this places on architects' consciousness and practices are significant. Working 'under neocapitalism', architects will inevitably produce and reproduce spaces that embody 'a close association [. . .] between daily reality (daily routine) and urban reality', within 'the routes and networks which link up the places set aside for work, "private" life and leisure' (38). While this might seem reasonable enough, or simply a reflection of practical reality, by reproducing the space(s) of neocapitalism, architects are destined to continuously establish 'the most extreme separation between the places' linked 'together' by the ever expanding networks and flows of global capitalism (38). More concretely, spaces for social life are almost impossible to achieve under these conditions.

Inevitably, the cultural dominant will seek to maintain a static condition of politics, economics and society, to say nothing of spatial practices. The limitations that this places on architects' consciousness and practices are significant.

In Lefebvre's view, the inextricable link between architects' working methods and the reproduction of spaces of the dominant authority is inevitable: 'The spatial practices of a society secretes that society's space' (38). While it might be possible that this supports the view of architects as determining spatial practices, this has repeatedly been shown not to be true, and at no time more so than the present: governments, the building industry, and commodity markets – the flows of capital – determine spatial practices to a far greater extent than architects have any hope of doing. The ubiquitous shopping mall, the generic café, economic pressures to use only standardised building products, the homogenising forces of regulation and framed curtain wall construction are some examples of this.

Repetition everywhere

Throughout Lefebvre's writing, the traditional city, in particular Italian cities including Siena, Florence and Rome, are returned to as counterexamples. Lefebvre asserts that '[t]here is no need to subject modern towns, their outskirts and new buildings, to careful scrutiny in order to reach the conclusion that everything here resembles everything else' (75). Such sameness analogises both abstraction and control, leading towards a degree of indistinguishability between architecture and the city that can seem pervasive:

> **The more or less accentuated split between what is known as 'architecture' and what is known as 'urbanism' – that is to say, between the 'micro' and 'macro' levels, and between these two areas of concern and the two professions concerned – has not resulted in an increased diversity. On the contrary. It is obvious, sad to say, that repetition has everywhere defeated uniqueness, that the artificial and contrived have driven all spontaneity and naturalness from the field, and, in short, that products have vanquished works.**

> **(75)**

However, the repetition that defeats the unique is not a consequence of incompetence, or even a poverty of imagination, but rather is rendered inevitable by a range of practices repeated without reflection, as much by architects as by the building industry they serve: 'Repetitious spaces are the outcome of repetitive gestures (those of the workers) associated with instruments which are both duplicatable and designed to duplicate: machines, bull-dozers, concrete-mixers, cranes, pneumatic drills, and so on' (75).

On the surface, the dominance of repetition could be construed as simply the product of atrophied imaginations. Such a view, though, holds the myth of expertise in reserve, while setting aside the possibility that it is *space as a product* – subject to economies of scale in production, reproducible and attaining its greatest value by being an exchangeable commodity – that overwhelms the use value of space. In this sense, the quantifiable trumps the qualitative: 'Are these spaces interchangeable because they are homologous? Or are they homogeneous so that they can be exchanged, bought and sold, with the only differences between them being those assessable in money – i.e. quantifiable – terms (as volumes, distances, etc.)?' (75). Whether or not one believes that repetition is a result of a certain similarity between these spaces or a requirement of their status as products, what is certain is that 'repetition reigns supreme' (75).

Lefebvre's distinction between 'works' and 'products' provides a helpful means for understanding the consequences of the repetitions that make space into product. Works achieve a status akin to works of art in the sense of being unique and not reproducible. On the other hand, products lend themselves to near infinite reproducibility by way of repetitive acts, akin to the production of any standardised item of exchange or consumption (70): 'Can a space of this kind really still be described as a "work". There is an overwhelming case for saying that it is a product *strictu sensu*: it is reproducible and it is the result of repetitive actions' (75). Although the production of space could appear to be applicable only at the scale of infrastructure or earthworks, in the sense of the massive transformations caused by such activities, Lefebvre argues that space can be considered to have been produced, or to be a product, at smaller scales as well: 'Thus space is undoubtedly produced even when the scale is not that of major highways, airports or public works' (75). In tandem with reproducibility, abstraction and quantifiability, the visual dominates in the realm of products, akin to the importance of package design in the appeal and sale of products:

> **A further important aspect of spaces of this kind is their increasingly pronounced visual character. They are made with the visible in mind: the visibility of people and things, of spaces and of whatever is contained by them. The predominance of visualization (more important than**

'Infinitely Reproducible', Sixth Avenue, New York City

'spectacularization', which is in any case subsumed by it) serves to conceal repetitiveness. People *look*, and take sight, take seeing, for life itself. We build on the basis of papers and plans. We buy on the basis of images.

(75–76)

As reflection on the dominance of transient fashion, appearance in architecture and the association between packaging and advertising readily reveals, the supremacy of the visual has a profoundly negative dimension: 'Sight and seeing, which in the Western tradition once epitomized intelligibility, have turned into a trap: the means whereby, in social space, diversity may be simulated and a travesty of enlightenment and intelligibility ensconced under the sign of transparency' (76). Recognising the association of transparency and display with the simulation of diversity is a crucial first step to developing an understanding of the link between modes of production, exchange value and the pervasiveness of spatial homogeneity; it could also be the first step to other spatial practices.

Lefebvre's distinction between 'works' and 'products' provides a helpful means for understanding the consequences of the repetitions that make space into product. Works achieve a status akin to works of art in the sense of being unique and not reproducible. On the other hand, products lend themselves to near infinite reproducibility.

Spatial codes

In Lefebvre's lexicon, a 'spatial code' is a 'system of space' that makes spaces legible to those who live within the culture that produced it. Although he is not confident that such a code exists in the present, he believes traces of one are discernible in the spatial practices of the Renaissance. In the event, '[i]f indeed spatial codes have existed, each characterizing a particular spatial/social practice, and if these codifications have been *produced* along with the space corresponding to them, then the job of theory is to elucidate their rise, their role, and their demise' (17). The value of identifying and deciphering codes, according to Lefebvre, resides in a shift of stress from the 'formal aspects of codes' to 'their dialectical character'. In this way, '[c]odes will be seen as part of a practical relationship' and 'as part of an interaction between "subjects" and their space and surroundings'. Continuing, Lefebvre describes his project, in relation to codes, as an 'attempt to trace the coming-into-being and disappearance of codings/decodings', which aims 'to highlight *contents* – i.e. the social (spatial) practices inherent to the forms under consideration' (18).

Although one might imagine such activities to be the very vocation of architects, in most instances, the dominance of visual and formal preoccupations precludes this. But it need not be thus. In fact, Lefebvre's attention to the potentially legible aspects of social and spatial practices that form spatial codes holds out the promise of modelling for architects an alternative manner of conceptualising their tasks. Setting the decoding of spatial codes as key to their work need not restrict architects' inventive capacities, but rather could return them to concrete considerations of the social dimensions of space. It is here that Renaissance spatial practices become particularly important, especially considering that, in Lefebvre's view, modernity (understood as a product of nineteenth- and twentieth-century developments) has included the destruction of generally legible spatial codes:

> **If, roughly from the sixteenth century to the nineteenth, a coded language may be said to have existed on the practical basis of a specific relationship between town, country and political territory, a language founded on classical perspective and Euclidean space, why and how did this coded system collapse? Should an attempt be made to reconstruct that language, which was common to the various groups making up the society – to users and inhabitants, to the authorities and to the technicians (architects, urbanists, planners)?**
>
> **(17, see also 47)**

Broadly speaking, Lefebvre's answer to the question he poses is 'no'. And yet there is a degree of lament in this; the fragmented spatial arrangements that we inhabit ultimately obstruct the emergence of a vital social life robust enough to counter the dominance of abstracting bureaucracies. The spatial conditions of the present have a reasonably long trajectory, but not so long that alternatives from the past have lost all resonance.

> The fact is that around 1910 a certain space was shattered. It was the space of common sense, of knowledge (*savoir*), of social practice, of political power, a space thitherto enshrined in everyday discourse, just as in abstract thought, as the environment of and channel for communications; the space, too, of classical perspective and geometry, developed from the Renaissance onwards on the basis of the Greek tradition (Euclid, logic) and bodied forth in Western art and philosophy, as in the form of the city and town.
>
> (25)

Fascinating in the preceding quote is Lefebvre's indication of the interdependency of space, mind and culture, in relation also to language, in determining the character of spatial practices and spaces. Thus, the shattering of the space inherited from the Renaissance presupposed the dissolution of a certain consciousness and its external manifestations as a particular kind of space; it was both dependent on this dissolution and a concretisation of it.

Consequently, although the loss of this space may be lamentable, it is equally irrecoverable in its exact form. Considering Lefebvre's assertion of the pre-modern city as a model superior to our own, its irretrievability raises an apparent paradox. Yet the enduring concrete presence of the counter-spaces of traditional cities, and the persistence of certain modes of social life habituated to them, suggests this apparent paradox can be resolved: the forms of the past are not simply nostalgic, they stand as a living critique of the present (a central theme of Lefebvre's thinking introduced earlier that is discussed further in the next chapter).

Nevertheless, Lefebvre asserts that the loss of the traditional space of the city must be acknowledged before alternatives can be arrived at: 'The fact remains that it is too late for destroying codes in the name of a critical theory; our task, rather, is to describe their already completed destruction, to measure its effects, and (perhaps) to construct a new code' (26). Lefebvre clarifies his initial doubts about spatial codes by suggesting that while their legibility is a 'logical necessity', they will likely only 'constitute a coherent whole' under promising conditions:

'Ancient Rome Intersects the Nineteenth-Century City', *Ponte Sisto* (1473–1479), from Trastevere across the Tiber to the *Centro Storico*, Rome, Italy

> That the lived, conceived and perceived realms should be interconnected, so that the 'subject', the individual member of a given social group, may move from one to another without confusion – so much is a logical necessity. Whether they constitute a coherent whole is another matter. They probably do so only in favourable circumstances, when a common language, a consensus and a code can be established.
>
> (40)

As has been introduced previously, for Lefebvre, such coherence emerged for Western towns during the Renaissance and endured until the nineteenth century, whence it was dissolved in the wake of industrialisation and the emergence of new spatial practices associated with capitalism:

> It is reasonable to assume that the Western town, from the Italian Renaissance to the nineteenth century, was fortunate enough to enjoy such auspicious conditions. [. . .] Tuscan painters, architects and theorists developed a representation of space – perspective – on the basis of a

> social practice which was itself [. . .] the result of a historic change in the
> relationship between town and country.
>
> **(40–41)**

Although the changes to social practices that made the Renaissance town
possible (which are mostly founded on 'representations of space' – perspective)
also resulted in a reduction of what Lefebvre calls the 'representational space
of religious origin' to 'symbolic figures', he asserts that 'representational space,
inherited from the Etruscans, which had survived all the centuries of Roman
and Christian dominance' was preserved 'virtually intact' (40, 41). Despite this
noteworthy survival of ancient social space, it is important to register Lefebvre's
ambivalence towards the crucial role of perspective in the emergence of the
Renaissance town:

> [T]he vanishing-point and the meeting of parallel lines 'at infinity' were
> the determinants of a representation, at once intellectual and visual, which
> promoted the primacy of the gaze in a kind of 'logic of visualization'. This
> representation, which had been in the making for centuries, now became
> enshrined in architectural and urbanistic practice as the *code* of linear perspective.
>
> **(41)**

Although linear perspective may no longer dominate in the way it once did, the
'logic of visualization' continues to prevail in architectural and urbanistic practice
to such a degree that, as noted previously, it has eclipsed the social dimension
of architecture and urbanism. Relative to this, Lefebvre asserts that an ideology
requires a space, or as he puts it: 'What is an ideology without a space to which
it refers, a space which it describes, whose vocabulary and links it makes use of,
and whose code it embodies?' (44). If this is accepted, then the current fashion
of thinking it safer to conceptualise architecture as empty, as a corrective to the
hubristic determinism of high modern architecture, is revealed as a significant
self-deception: spatial practices are inevitably ideologically coded. Indeed, if
architecture were actually empty that would arguably have much more to do
with a wider trend of vacuousness than with any ideological void or putative

autonomy. Rather, social and political life (and the architecture it describes and gives a form) devoid of some ideology is a necessary adjunct of consensus. Understood in this way, rather than being genuinely autonomous, an architecture which has abdicated from the task of social dreaming actually bolsters a culture hostile to the possibilities of alternative spaces. Indeed, such spaces are implicated in the reproduction of the – often quite vacant – prevailing system of dominant beliefs that organises everyday life. Lefebvre observes that a reconstructed spatial code is a necessary precursor to a different space, and with it a different life:

> The reconstruction of a spatial 'code' – that is, of a language common to practice and theory, as also to inhabitants, architects and scientists – may be considered from the practical point of view to be an immediate task. The first thing such a code would do is recapture the unity of dissociated elements, breaking down such barriers as that between private and public, and identifying both confluences and oppositions in space that are at present indiscernible.
>
> **(64)**

The current fashion of thinking it safer to conceptualise architecture as empty, as a corrective to the hubristic determinism of high modern architecture, is revealed as a significant self-deception: spatial practices are inevitably ideologically coded.

The link between fragmentation in the urban environment and the divisions of capitalism is not, according to Lefebvre, simply coincidental. In fact, the association is inevitable. Thus, a truly alternative space and life would necessarily entail recapturing 'the unity of dissociated elements' (64). The new code leading to the emergence of such new conditions:

> would thus bring together levels and terms which are isolated by existing spatial practice and by the ideologies underpinning it: the 'micro' or architectural level and the 'macro' level currently treated as the province of urbanists, politicians and planners; the everyday realm and the urban realm; inside and outside; work and non-work (festival); the durable and the ephemeral; and so forth.
>
> (64)

The bringing together of terms at present rigidly isolated from one another by dualistic oppositions set up between them has very little to do with erasing *difference*. Rather, the aim would be to create a new code in which apparent social and spatial oppositions could coexist, while maintaining their respective difference.

> The code would therefore comprise significant oppositions (i.e. paradigmatic elements) to be found amidst seemingly disparate terms, and links (syntagmatic elements) retrieved from the seemingly homogeneous mass of politically controlled space. In this sense the code might be said to contribute to the reversal of the dominant tendency and thus to play a role in the overall project.
>
> (64)

Of equal importance to accommodating apparent oppositions, the code Lefebvre envisions is not intended to be a method or a specific mode of practice, but rather a way of conceptualising and communicating a recuperated coherence. As such, this new code must be aligned to practice, to maintain its connection to concrete conditions and also to prevent it from drifting into abstraction:

> It is vital, however, that the code itself not be mistaken for a practice. The search for a language must therefore in no circumstances be permitted to become detached from practice or from the changes wrought by practice (i.e. from the worldwide process of transformation).
>
> (64–65)

Practice – the concrete – is the inescapable context of Lefebvre's thinking, which is why it is not surprising that the earliest spatial code he could identify was outlined by the first-century BC Roman architect Marcus Vitruvius Pollio (better known as Vitruvius) in his *Ten Books on Architecture*:

> Truth to tell, the first formulation of such a unitary code dates back to antiquity, and specifically to Vitruvius. The work of the Roman architect contains an elaborate attempt to establish term-by-term correspondences between the various elements of social life in the context of a particular spatial practice, that of a builder working in a city that he knows from the inside.
>
> **(270)**

Although Lefebvre is impressed by the thoroughness of what he calls Vitruvius's 'treatise on spatial semiology', he identifies one significant absence: 'The city in Vitruvius is conspicuous by its absence/presence; though he is speaking of nothing else, he never addresses it directly' (271). Importantly, however, the absence of the city as a specific topic for Vitruvius has less to do with an oversight on his part than with the relative contiguity of city and country that persisted from the emergence of cities until the close of the medieval period, when towns 'emerge as a unified entity and as a *subject*' (271). Paradoxically, it was at this time that the urban and rural were thought to form a unity: 'Together with its territory, the Renaissance town perceived itself as a harmonious whole, as an organic mediation between earth and heaven' (271). As it turns out, by the end of the nineteenth century, this nearly utopian association – between what is now mostly conceived of as an opposition – was shattered 'under the impact of industrialization and' the rise of the state (272).

Spatial practice/representations of space/representational space

The idea of describing space as a product, which is normally associated with something tangible or concrete, might seem to defy understanding, especially because space is generally understood as infinite, or as an abstraction.

However, Lefebvre's aim is to reveal the degree to which the space of a specific culture is a product of its unique spatial practices, and that these are inextricably bound to the modes of production of that particular society. In this way *space* can be understood as tangible, as producible or reproducible, as a product. Lefebvre explains his understanding of space as product as follows:

> [E]very society – and hence every mode of production [. . .] produces a space, its own space. The city of the ancient world cannot be understood as a collection of people and things in space; nor can it be visualized solely on the basis of a number of texts and treatises on the subject of space. [. . .] For the ancient city had its own spatial practice: it forged its own – *appropriated* – space. Whence the need for a study of that space which is able to apprehend it as such, in its genesis and its form, with its own specific time or times (the rhythm of daily life), and its particular centres and polycentrism (agora, temple, stadium, etc.). [. . .] Schematically speaking, each society offers up its own peculiar space, as it were, as an 'object' for analysis and overall theoretical explication. I say each society, but it would be more accurate to say each mode of production, along with its specific relations of production.
>
> (31)

Lefebvre emphasises here the degree to which space, although initially conceptualised as abstract, has a specific character dependent on the time and place of its emergence, and is linked to 'specific relations of production' (31). Equally, he binds particular modes of production to a specific society. In localising space, Lefebvre immediately challenges ideas of it as empty and infinite, rather than determinate and populated by people and things. In this way, the space described by Lefebvre is ultimately 'social space': the space of production, relations of production and of individual and group life: 'In reality, social space "incorporates" social actions, the actions of subjects, both individual and collective who are born and who die, who suffer and who act' (33).

> Lefebvre's aim is to reveal the degree to which the space of a specific culture is a product of its unique spatial practices, and that these are inextricably bound to the modes of production of that particular society.

Social space and its understanding takes three principal forms, described by Lefebvre as 'spatial practice', 'representations of space' and 'representational spaces'. As defined by Lefebvre, 'spatial practice [. . .] embraces production and reproduction, and the particular locations and spatial sets characteristic of each social formation'. As such, '[s]patial practice', according to Lefebvre, 'ensures continuity and some degree of [social and spatial] cohesion' (33). Such cohesion is crucial because it 'implies a guaranteed level of *competence* and a specific level of *performance*' relative to 'social space, and of each member of a given society's relationship to that space' (33). Spatial practice is a form of social practice that Lefebvre argues is 'lived directly before it is conceptualized' (34). In this regard, Lefebvre reminds the reader that his focus is on the concrete, and on practices, rather than on the abstract or the theoretical. However, as a directly lived social practice, '[i]n *spatial practice*, the reproduction of social relations is predominant' (50). If this is to be accepted, it returns the discussion to just how difficult it is to break free from reproducing what already is, even in the most apparently radical architecture and urbanism.

In ancient Rome, 'spatial practice' took two main forms: 'the Roman road, whether civil or military, links the *urbs* [the urban], to the countryside over which it exercises dominion. The road allows the city, as people and as Senate, to assert its political centrality at the core of the *orbis terrarium* [the rural ground]'. In addition to the road, the 'gate, through which the imperial way proceeds from *urbs* to *orbis*, marks the sacrosanct enceinte [enclosing wall] off from its subject territories, and allows for entrance and exit'. As a kind of counterbalance to the road and gate, as manifestations of Roman control, there is 'the pole of "private" life, juridicially established in the heart of "political" society, and according to the same principles, those of property – we find the Roman house, a response to clearly defined needs' (245). In short, ancient Roman spatial practices resulted in clear expressions of Roman domination; demarcation of who is and who is not a Roman; and also private life as a counterweight to the reach of Rome.

According to Lefebvre, 'representations of space [. . .] are tied to the relations of production and to the "order" which those relations impose, and hence to knowledge, to signs, to codes, and to "frontal" relations' (33). More explicitly, 'representations of space' are 'conceptualized space, the space of scientists, planners, urbanists, technocratic subdividers and social engineers, as of a certain type of artist with a scientific bent – all of whom identify what is lived and what is perceived with what is conceived' (38). Putting it more succinctly, 'representations of space' are abstractions or intellectualisations of lived space. As such, the dynamism of concrete experience is muted by attempts to codify it, or transform it into an easily read sign. In Lefebvre's view, and in consideration of the dominance of abstraction, '[t]his is the dominant space in any society (or mode of production)', inasmuch as 'established relations between objects and people in represented space' analogise the divisions of the dominant social (spatial) practices (39, 41).

Lefebvre observes that 'representations of space' are the province of producers, of architects for example, who have in mind the production of a specific kind of space identified with a particular ideology, limited by the 'relations of production' at a given time and in a particular place (42, 43, 46, 77). If those experts responsible for the production of space operate with abstract representations of space in mind, and these are ultimately constructed, it is no wonder that a wide gap generally exists between their claims for these spaces and the way spaces are actually lived, which also begins to clarify the sources of the widespread failure of modern spaces, that largely reproduce the shattering of pre-modern space out of which they arise.

It is important to keep in mind that, although Lefebvre's consideration of 'representations of space' inevitably includes architectural representations, his main point is to suggest that there is a dominant representation of space in circulation at any given moment – in any particular context – that will largely determine the production of space in that particular context (social, political, economic) (38–47). For example, Lefebvre argues that in ancient Rome, the dominant representation was of '*orbis* and the *urbs*, circular, with their extensions and implications (arch, vault)' on the one hand, and 'on the other hand the military camp with its strict grid and its two perpendicular axes, *cardo* and *decumanus* – a closed space, set apart and fortified' (245).

Lefebvre asserts that the third part of his triad, 'representational spaces', embody 'complex symbolisms, sometimes coded, sometimes not, linked to the clandestine or underground side of social life, as also to art (which may come eventually to be defined less as a code of space than as a code of representational spaces)' (33). But it also relates this category to the spaces of religion. According to Lefebvre, representational space is:

> directly *lived* through its associated images and symbols, and hence is the space of 'inhabitants' and 'users', but also of some artists and perhaps of those, such as a few writers and philosophers, who *describe* and aspire to do no more than describe. This is the dominated – and hence passively experienced – space which the imagination seeks to change and appropriate. It overlays physical space, making symbolic use of its objects.
>
> (39)

Clarifying somewhat, Lefebvre continues: 'representational spaces may be said [. . .] to tend towards more or less coherent systems of non-verbal symbols and signs' (39). Such spaces are also 'redolent with imaginary and symbolic elements' that 'have their source in history – in the history of a people as well as in the history of each individual belonging to that people' (41).

In the way Lefebvre explains it, 'representational spaces' are the most significant symbolic spaces within a village or town primarily for inhabitants (rather than the state): 'Representational spaces [. . .] determined the foci of a vicinity: the village church, graveyard, hall and fields, or the square and the belfry. Such spaces were interpretations, sometimes marvellously successful ones, of cosmological representations' (45). As such, these spaces transact in the magical (or perhaps better to say mysterious) and the qualitative, rather than in the scientific and the quantitative. Continuing with Rome as an example, Lefebvre explains that its 'representational spaces' were 'dual in character' including 'the masculine principle, military, authoritarian, juridical – and dominant; and the feminine, which, though not denied, is integrated, thrust down into the "abyss" of the earth, as the place where seeds are sown and the dead are laid, as "world" ' (245). In this arrangement, the ostensible chthonian feminine principles counterbalance the priapic masculine ones, promising both the purging of the world and its rebirth. Although not rational in a sense that moderns might expect, having spaces dedicated to presumed masculine and feminine principles analogised a certain cosmic balance. Finally, in Lefebvre's terms, the 'perceived – conceived – [directly] lived [or experienced] triad' correlates, in the realm of space, to 'spatial practice, representations of space' and 'representational spaces' (40, 246).

'Chthonian Feminine Principles Counterbalance the Priapic Masculine Ones', *Foro Romano*, Rome, Italy

The antithesis of systems

Lefebvre's main objective, then, is not an operative theory – 'directed at space itself', nor at the construction of 'models, typologies or prototypes of spaces' – that can be easily instrumentalised but 'an exposition of the *production of space*' (404). Because he is fundamentally opposed to system-building (the assertion of an all-encompassing network of explanations), which he sees as a direct expression of power, of abstraction and of reductionism, he inevitably does not propose specific (supposedly ameliorating) results. While this can be frustrating for architects, who are understandably anxious to know how theories can be put to work, or, at the very least, how they can assist in completing design tasks, it is precisely this reluctance to propose specific results that assures the enduring generative capacities of Lefebvre's ideas. The basic principles, or suggestive outlines, of the sort of mental framework and atmosphere of what Lefebvre encourages as counter-projects, counter-proposals and counter-spaces are there. The specifics, however, remain the task of individuals and communities to invent. Succinctly, their task is the shift from a 'problematic of space' to 'spatial practices' (414).

Because he is fundamentally opposed to system-building (the assertion of an all-encompassing network of explanations), which he sees as a direct expression of power, of abstraction and of reductionism, he inevitably does not propose specific (supposedly ameliorating) results.

The alternative approach Lefebvre encourages would throw into question 'the primacy of the visual realm [. . . ,] images and [the] graphic dimension, [as well as] the phallic (military and heroic) principle, which belongs, as one of its chief properties, to abstract space' (408). According to him the space he criticises overuses 'straight lines, right angles, and strict (rectilinear) perspective', manifesting what he calls 'masculine virtues which gave rise to domination by this space', leading 'to a generalized state of deprivation' (410). However, Lefebvre is quick to acknowledge that articulating counter-proposals and realising them is no easy task:

> The obstacles faced by counter-plans may be enumerated. The most serious is the fact that on one side, the side of power, there are ranged resources and strategies on a vast scale – the scale, ultimately, of the planet – while in opposition to these forces stand only the limited knowledge and limited interests of generally medium-sized or small territorial spheres. [. . .] All the same, the necessary inventiveness can only spring from interaction between plans and counter-plans, projects and counter-projects. (Not that such interaction should be seen as excluding ripostes *in kind* to the violence of established political powers.)
>
> **(419)**

Here again is an assertion of Lefebvre's unique optimism, which turns on his conviction that it is only through encounters with existing reality – 'between plans and counter-plans, projects and counter-projects' – that proposals for surpassing that reality, for escaping its domination, can be invented. In this way, Lefebvre avoids the impasse presented by Tafuri (introduced in earlier chapters), without defaulting to the formalism (as a preoccupation with supposedly autonomous visual and spatial forms conceived in isolation from social and political contexts) encouraged by architectural critic Colin Rowe (1920–1999) and so many current practitioners.

However, architects, planners and developers are not likely to welcome the nature of the counter-plans and counter-projects encouraged by Lefebvre, which presuppose 'a collective ownership and [self-] management of space [of territorial units, towns, urban communities, regions and so on] founded on the permanent participation of the "interested parties", with their multiple, varied and even contradictory interests. It thus also presupposes confrontation' (416,

422). By the same token, the counter-projects potentially stimulated by Lefebvre would be founded on an orientation:

> to surpass separations and dissociations, notably those between the *work* (which is unique: an object bearing the stamp of a 'subject', of the creator or artist, and of a single, unrepeatable moment) and the *product* (which is repeatable: the result of repetitive gestures, hence reproducible, and capable ultimately of bringing about the automatic reproduction of social relationships).

> **(422)**

In a world dominated by the language of 'brands' and 'icons', not least in discussions of buildings and cities (and even of the self), an ideology of *originality* raises a paradoxical conflict: ostensible *works* quickly become *products*, their putative 'icon' status being based on their 'brand recognition'. Ultimately, *reproducibility* trumps actual *uniqueness*. Consider as examples the proliferation of structures by Santiago Calatrava, Norman Foster, Daniel Libeskind or numerous other readily identifiable architect names. Counter-projects would not only negate or transcend the logic of 'brands' and 'icons'; they would escape the conceptual limits (mirrored by linguistic limits) such ways of thinking places upon the task of architecture.

In a world dominated by the language of 'brands' and 'icons', not least in discussions of buildings and cities (and even of the self), an ideology of *originality* raises a paradoxical conflict: ostensible *works* quickly become *products*, their putative 'icon' status being based on their 'brand recognition'.

As suggested earlier, Lefebvre's counter-projects represent a challenge of a utopian sort. The importance of reasserting this aspect of his thinking

Sage Gateshead, Gateshead, UK, Foster + Partners, Architects (1997–2004)

throughout the present study turns on the degree to which rejection of Utopia is even today accepted as quite reasonable, as closed, without the requirement of any further discussion. But the embrace of such a position threatens to nullify Lefebvre's thought as well. In the last pages of *The Production of Space*, Lefebvre reaffirms the undeniable utopianness of his project:

> On the horizon, then, at the furthest edge of the possible, it is a matter of producing the space of the human species – the collective (generic) work of the species – on the model of what used to be called 'art'; indeed, it is still so called, but art no longer has any meaning at the level of an 'object' isolated by and for the individual.
>
> (422)

Lefebvre's counter-description of art as a non-commoditised *work* of relevance for individuals in an engaged way is intriguing, more so because he asserts that 'the space of the human species' should be produced on this model of art. His location of such a possibility 'on the horizon, [. . .] at the furthest edge of the possible' is of even greater interest; where else is this but Utopia (422)?

> **The creation (or production) of a planet-wide space as the social foundation of a transformed everyday life open to myriad possibilities – such is the dawn now beginning to break on the far horizon. This is the same dawn as glimpsed by the great Utopians (who, inasmuch as they demonstrated real possibilities, are perhaps not properly so described): by Fourier, Marx and Engels, whose dreams and imaginings are as stimulating to theoretical thought as their concepts.**
>
> **(422–423)**

But this is not the totalising Utopia of blueprints imposed from above so often associated with the failures of the modern movement of architecture (the utopianness of which is, at any rate, mostly questionable, except in the most negative sense). Nor is it the Utopia of impossibility or fanciful, though unrealisable, visions; rather, it is a Utopia of real projects reliant on an 'orientation' rather than a 'system' for their (relative) emergence:

> **I speak of an orientation advisedly. We are concerned with nothing more and nothing less than that. We are concerned with what might be called a 'sense': an organ that perceives, a direction that may be conceived and a directly lived movement progressing towards the horizon. And we are concerned with nothing that even remotely resembles a system.**
>
> **(423)**

This last point is crucial: because of its association with supposedly logical teleological processes that are inevitably reductive and contribute to alienation, system-building is to be avoided at all costs. Thus, the length and breadth of *The Production of Space* is directly related to a mode of analysis and its presentation that reveals the reunion of two things usually maintained as separate and all but irreconcilable: *form* and *content*. If Lefebvre's book – its content – develops a challenge to the abstract and reductive presentation of reality that making systems requires, its presentation – form – militates against the easy systematisation of his thinking from beginning to end. Easy utopias demand the violence of reduction; utopias of transformation inevitably lend themselves to no such schematising methodisation.

CHAPTER 4

Rhythmanalysis and the timespace of the city

> At no moment have the analysis of rhythms and the rhythmanalytical project
> lost sight of the body. Not the anatomical or functional body, but the body
> as polyrhythmic and eurhythmic. [. . .] As such, the living body has [. . .]
> always been present: a constant reference. The theory of rhythms is founded
> on the experience and knowledge [. . .] of the body; the concepts derive
> from this consciousness and this knowledge, simultaneously banal and full of
> surprises – of the unknown and the misunderstood.
>
> (Lefebvre 2004 [1992]: 67)

> Henceforth, you will grasp every being [. . .], every entity [. . .] and every
> body, both living and non-living, 'symphonically', or 'polyrhythmically'.
> You will grasp it in its space-time, in its place and its approximate becoming:
> including houses and buildings, towns and landscapes.
>
> (Lefebvre and Régulier 2004 [1985]: 80)

Throughout this book the central themes of Lefebvre's thinking have been
considered in an attempt to show the continuing relevance of his work
for imagining alternatives to the spaces of neoliberal consensus. Lefebvre's
enrichments of Marxism are key for transforming his theories into localised
(rather than totalising) practices that resist state and corporate domination of
space while encouraging the production of places for individual and group
sociability. Ultimately, making architecture, or producing urban space, with
Lefebvre must resist depoliticising him if real change is the aim. However,
because architecture's existence depends on the very sorts of systems that
Lefebvre confronts, its fundamentally conservative position requires that
his thinking be sanitised. In response to this tendency, geographer Stuart
Elden argues:

there is a great danger that [Lefebvre] is reduced to being [. . .]
appropriated [. . .] to lend support to another 'postmodern'
project [. . .] without due regard for [his] theoretical basis or political
[convictions]. [. . .] [T]his does Lefebvre a great disservice: his political
edge is blunted and his philosophical complexity denied. [. . .] Lefebvre's
work needs to be understood in the context of his Marxism and of
philosophy more generally. [. . .] Understanding Lefebvre's work on space
within this wider context returns to this thinker the subtlety, complexity
and radical nature he deserves.

(Elden 2001: 809, 810)

In architecture, the depoliticisation of Lefebvre's thinking is inevitable because
there is a certain danger inherent to engaging in explicitly Marxist critiques of
architecture production after the fall of the Berlin Wall in 1989, and with it the
apparent demise of a socialist project, both of which predate the appearance
of *The Production of Space* in English translation in 1991 (Stanek 2011: 1–2).
As a corrective, this book offers possible ways for expanding the horizons of
Lefebvre's applicability that do not do violence to his radical convictions. Even
so, the conundrum of applying Lefebvre's thinking to architecture remains. Its
enclosure by capitalism, with its propensity for destroying communities, presents
the biggest obstacle.

Lefebvre's ambivalence towards Le Corbusier (1887–1965) is helpful for
discerning what might constitute a Lefebvrian architecture in cities, as opposed to
what would not. On the one hand, Lefebvre describes Le Corbusier's city plans as
promulgating a project for 'abstract and Cartesian' space, inevitably destructive
of difference and thus also of social life, which makes the plans homologous
with the aims of the state. On the other hand, Lefebvre considered Le Corbusier
'a genius' and a 'good architect', even though a 'catastrophic urbanist' (Lefebvre
1972; 1996 [1986]: 207). The divide he observed in Le Corbusier separates the
architect's theory – seen as overly certain, rigid and lacking vitality – from his
architectural practice, the actual buildings, seen as 'more hesitant, more flexible
and more vital' (Lefebvre 1972). This appreciation of Le Corbusier's architectural

practices, counterbalanced by a rejection of his urbanism and theory, is supported by most histories of twentieth-century architecture and urbanism. As arguably amongst the most important theorists of modern spatial practices, Lefebvre's take on 'the most celebrated architect and town planner of modern time', as he called Le Corbusier, is of significant interest (Lefebvre 1972).

A resolution of the schism that Lefebvre identifies between *city* and *building* in Le Corbusier's theory and practice is suggested in the work of Dutch artist Constant Nieuwenhuys (1920–2005) and his associations with the Situationist International (SI) (1957–1972), and with Dutch architect Aldo van Eyck (1918–1999) (Boersma 2005; Coleman 2005; Heynen 1999: 151–174; Strauven 1998). Lefebvre's own interactions with the SI are also suggestive of this (Ross 1997 [1983]). However, van Eyck's influence on Le Corbusier's unbuilt Venice Hospital project (1964) shows how even this so-called catastrophic urbanist made attempts in his own work to resolve the dichotomy between architecture and urbanism in something of a Lefebvrian register (Coleman 2005: 18–19; Sarkis 2001). Ultimately, van Eyck's association with Nieuwenhuys suggests that he was – at least in spirit – a *Lefebvrian* architect; a claim supported by the expanded imaginary of van Eyck's work on the problematic of architecture and urbanism, in particular his conviction that both could become *counterforms* to everyday life in the modern world.

In terms of attempting to make Lefebvre's ideas on architecture and the city operational, van Eyck's architecture and urbanism is extremely valuable, even though the two men appear never to have met. Van Eyck was, and remains, a contentious figure in architecture, which is precisely what makes him and his work a good example of how Lefebvre's ideas could take an architectural *counterform*. Arguably, this contentiousness turns on precisely those preoccupations he shared with Lefebvre, relative to the poverty of architecture and the cities it produces in the modern world. Like Lefebvre, van Eyck (whose last building was completed in 1997) continues to offer architects and urbanists ways of thinking alternatives, with a set of tools for imagining *counter-practices* to the mainstream of production. As this chapter will develop, van Eyck was one

'*Counterforms* to Everyday Life', Amsterdam Orphanage, Amstelveenseweg, Amsterdam (1955–1960), Aldo van Eyck, Architect

of very few post–World War II architects consistently preoccupied with concerns analogous to those central to Lefebvre's enterprise.

Rhythmanalysis and different spaces

Perhaps of all of Lefebvre's key concepts – including his 'theory of moments' (in which a specific occasion of limited duration latent in the everyday disrupts its continuousness by introducing otherness and the possibility of radical transformation into it, festivals being an example of this); the 'possible-impossible'; 'transduction'; and 'differential space' (the opposite of abstract space, albeit nascent in it) – it is 'rhythmanalysis' that is most relevant for the elaboration of alternative modes of architectural practice. Near the conclusion of *The Production of Space*, Lefebvre explains just why rhythmanalysis is crucial for the invention of different spaces:

> The genesis of a far-away order can be accounted for only on the basis of the order that is nearest to us – namely, the order of the body. Within the body itself, spatially considered, the successive levels constituted by the senses (from the sense of smell to sight treated as different within a differentiated field) prefigure the layers of social space and their interconnections. The passive body (the senses) and the active body (labour) converge in space. The analysis of rhythms must serve the necessary and inevitable restoration of the total body. This is what makes 'rhythm analysis' so important.
>
> (Lefebvre 1991 [1974]: 405)

The counter-spaces of a far-away order, inevitably associated with utopias, begin with the body, the *total body*, which Lefebvre believes only a *rhythmanalysis* can recuperate. Because it is precisely the 'genesis of' just such 'a far-away' order that recommends Lefebvre as a thinker for architects, in what follows, the relevance of rhythmanalysis for the invention of a non-hegemonic architecture is considered in some detail. Although first published posthumously in France in 1992, and in English translation in 2004 as part of the collection *Rhythmanalysis: Space, Time and Everyday Life*, Lefebvre's final book, *Elements of Rhythmanalysis: An Introduction to Understanding Rhythms*, is the culmination of ideas on rhythms that suffuse much of his work, including specific articles on the topic published as early as 1985. *Rhythmanalysis* contains his most sustained consideration of the topic. The English-language version includes two of the earlier essays on the topic, written with his last wife, Catherine Régulier. Lefebvre's aim in developing the method of 'rhythmanalysis' was 'nothing less than to found a science, a new field of knowledge', characterised, obviously enough, by the 'analysis of rhythms', which he argued would have 'practical consequences' (Lefebvre 2004 [1992]: 3).

The counter-spaces of a far-away order, inevitably associated with utopias, begin with the body, the *total body*, which Lefebvre believes only a *rhythmanalysis* can recuperate.

Rephrasing ideas on a method he had been developing for some time, Lefebvre argues that in conducting a rhythmanalysis, rather than 'going from the concrete to the abstract', the rhythmanalyst starts with 'concepts' and 'definite categories', 'with full consciousness of the abstract to arrive at the concrete'. Although an ostensibly risky procedure, for its apparent irrationality, this way of conducting analysis encourages 'speculation in the place of analysis, the *arbitrarily* subjective in the place of facts' (Lefebvre 2004 [1992]: 5). The wider value of this decidedly open process, and of rhythmanalysis in particular, is that it offers a defence against totalising thought without doing violence to experience: 'The spectre of theoretical questioning goes from *pure* abstraction [. . .] to the full complexity of the contradictions of the *real*' (Lefebvre 2004 [1992]: 13).

Lefebvre went to great lengths to defend against the confusion of '*rhythm* with *movement*' (Lefebvre 2004 [1992]: 5). In his terms, *movement* is regularised to such a degree that it is certain, leaving little or no possibility for difference to emerge, which *rhythm* always permits; 'there is always something new and unforeseen that introduces itself into the repetitive: difference' (Lefebvre 2004 [1992]: 5). The difference is between machine-like *movement* and the more nuanced character of *measure* that is significant here: *measure* always refers back to the body whereas the metronomic movements of machines are antithetical to it, ultimately deforming the body to mechanistic requirements. Even so, the two are 'reciprocal [. . .] they measure themselves against one another; [. . .] everything is cyclical repetition through linear repetitions' (Lefebvre 2004 [1992]: 8). According to Lefebvre, 'harmony [. . .] is simultaneously quantitative and qualitative (in music and elsewhere; language, movements, architecture [. . .], etc.)' (Lefebvre 2004 [1992]: 8).

Lefebvre's preoccupation with rhythm, however, has little or nothing to do with the elements that make up a building, or adorn its façade, except inasmuch as these characteristics analogise the bodies and social activities of the individuals or groups who might inhabit both buildings and urban settings. Moreover, the rhythmic, the cyclical:

> originates in the cosmic, in nature: days, nights, seasons, the waves and tides of the sea, monthly cycles, etc. [. . .] Great cyclical rhythms last for a period and restart: dawn is always new. [. . .] The antagonistic unity of relations between the cyclical sometimes gives rise to compromises, sometimes to disturbances. [. . .] Not only does repetition not exclude differences, it also gives birth to them: it *produces* them.
>
> (Lefebvre 2004 [1992]: 7)

Lefebvre argues that rhythmanalysis returns the body to consciousness. As such its greatest potential contribution to the theory and practice of architecture is to re-propose the body as a referent in all works: the organisation of the body, its scale and its rhythms as well (internal functioning and habits alike).

Above all else, the body is the final referent in Lefebvre's exposition of rhythmanalysis, which offers an important lesson for architects, specifically: although the built environment will inevitably be populated by bodies, buildings and urban settings can often seem indifferent to the facts of the body – social and individual alike. Lefebvre does not explicitly criticise architects for this oversight, but he surely implies it: 'Rhythm appears as regulated time, governed by rational laws, but in contact with what is least rational in human being: the lived, the carnal, the body (Lefebvre 2004 [1992]: 9). Bodies embody rhythms, and are the model for them. Perhaps the absence of the lived body from architectural imaginings in the present has something to do with the persisting dominance of science and technology in shaping consciousness in our epoch, evident for example in the logic of *planning* or *human resources* as regimes of management control that regularise and depersonalise.

Along these lines, Lefebvre reflected: 'It used to be thought that science and technology suffice. Yet, necessary and non-sufficient, science and technology pose the problem of all problems. An absolute problem: What can philosophy do? Perceive the situation? Appreciate the risk? Point a way out?' (Lefebvre

2004 [1992]: 14) The continuing incapacity of architecture and urbanism to provide suitable settings for social relations in the modern world arguably reflects the persisting pseudo-scientific (rationalist, reductionist) aspirations of many practitioners. But in the invention and provision of buildings and cities, neither science nor art, as autonomous from social life and bodies, is sufficient. Rather, the answer resides with the body: 'Delving further into the hypothesis [that although necessary, science and technology are not sufficient], **rhythm** (linked on the one hand to logical categories and mathematical calculations – and on the other to the visceral and vital body) would hold the secrets and the answer to strange questions', for example: what can philosophy do? (Lefebvre 2004 [1992]: 14). In this instance I would like to associate architecture with philosophy and ask: what can architecture do?

Collapsing dualities

Lefebvre's collapse of rigid oppositions between apparent dualities, his concept of rhythm and his conviction that science and technology do not have all the answers are mirrored in a number of van Eyck's ideas on architecture. In particular, his concepts of 'twinphenomena' and the 'in-between', as necessary double conditions and interstitial spaces respectively, have an affinity with Lefebvre's approach.

Lefebvre's collapse of rigid oppositions between apparent dualities, his concept of rhythm and his conviction that science and technology do not have all the answers are mirrored in a number of van Eyck's ideas on architecture.

For van Eyck, 'twinphenomena' are emotional states or building components that are made out of interdependently associated elements apparently opposed to one another (Coleman 2005: 209–233). Van Eyck clarifies this as a coexistence of 'unity and diversity, part and whole, small and large, many and few, simplicity and complexity, change and constancy, order and chaos, individual and collective' (van Eyck 1993 [1962]: 348). When an accord between apparent opposites is acknowledged in the arrangement of buildings (including the elements out of which they are made and the accommodation they house) or urban settings, the potential for a greater affinity with the constructed environment emerges, precisely because closeness between building and body is achieved through what van Eyck calls 'harmony in motion' (or 'dynamic equilibrium') (van Eyck 1993 [1962]: 353). Twinphenomena are, for van Eyck, primarily related by in-betweens, which are counterforms of human ambivalence that can contain and assuage it by accommodating both-and conditions that confound dualities (the architectural correlate of which is thresholds of all kinds) (van Eyck 1993 [1962]: 348). As a setting, the 'in-between' is a potential site of subversiveness precisely because the positive rendering of the gaps it describes simultaneously links and separates opposed conditions in just the ways that overly rationalised buildings and cities attempt to erase (Coleman 2005: 196–233).

Arguably, van Eyck engaged in a sort of rhythmanalysis in the development of the concepts introduced earlier, and in others as well, including what he called the 'problem of vast number', which relates to the use of repeating structural elements in modern assembled (industrialised) construction. The lack of consideration given to the problem of repetitive elements in modern construction tends to defeat the intelligibility of the constructed environment. According to van Eyck, the corrective for this problem is to apply what he called 'laws of dynamic equilibrium' to the design and construction of buildings. If initial elements can be made to withstand repetition, individual and particular elements would achieve enrichment by continuously reasserting their identity throughout the collection of parts assembled into a generalised whole. Van Eyck named this give and take between part and whole 'harmony in motion', which operates according to what he called the 'laws of dynamic equilibrium': a balanced tuning of elements that imparts 'rhythm to repetitive similar and dissimilar forms'. Taken together, all of the various parts of building, if arranged in the manner proposed by van Eyck, would constitute a complex whole that is simultaneously a collective, plural and general. Ultimately, although van Eyck's approach to architecture results in agreeable built forms, it was primarily a method for achieving a more humane built environment, inasmuch as the application of his innovations promised a range of settings – from house to city – that would be far more responsive to the complexity of individual and social bodies than the hyper-rationality of orthodox modern architecture and urbanism could ever be (Coleman 2005: 16–23, 99–111, 196–233, 242–258).

Van Eyck's approach is dialectical, in much the way Lefebvre's method is. For Lefebvre, the conventional understanding of the world as a collection of rigid oppositions, in which, for example, the *ideal* and the *real* must forever remain separate, deprives theory, research and practice of a powerful tool for drawing something new out of the given. His dialectical method, which he calls 'triadic analysis', offers a way to think towards the possible: to what appears impossible in the context of dualistic thinking, but which a dialectical mind-set can begin to bring within reach:

> It is only recently, with Hegel and Marx, that analysis has understood the triadic character of the approach by becoming dialectical in accordance with the scheme: *thesis-antithesis-synthesis*. [. . .] [D]ialectical analysis constitutes the relations between three terms, which change according to circumstance: going from conflict to alliance and back again. This in the presence of the world, to the extent that it features relations of past-present-future, or of possible-probable-impossible. [. . .] The analysis does not isolate an object or a subject, or a relation. It seeks to grasp a moving but determinate complexity. [. . .] It doesn't lead to *synthesis* in accordance with the Hegelian schema. [. . .] Thus the triad [. . .] links three terms that it leaves distinct, without fusing them. [. . .] The dialectic proclaims 'There is neither thought nor reality without contradictions.'
>
> (Lefebvre 2004 [1992]: 11–13)

Lefebvre's understanding of dialectics as a 'triadic analysis', in which three terms are linked but maintain their individual identity, mounts significant resistance to dualistic rationality, in which apparent opposites are maintained as separate or conflicting to uphold mental or organisational clarity. The association between the terms, according to him, is more relational; contradictions (or complexity) are tolerated, and synthesis is not the aim, nor is the reductive isolation of specific elements or aspects of the object of analysis. Lefebvre's characterisation of 'triadic analysis' finds its clearest architectural correlation in van Eyck's work, as described earlier. Most concretely, van Eyck does not attempt to resolve opposites in his buildings (inside and outside for example) through synthesis, but rather makes a virtue of their coexistence (as twinphenomena) mediated by the in-between, as a third condition. While this describes his architectural language, it also refers to his conviction that twinphenomena in built work can best accommodate contradictions in social relations, including the human condition of ambivalence. The value of triadic analysis for the invention of architecture and urban settings in the present derives from the counter-position to reductionism it articulates: the more architecture can come to terms with the inevitability of contradiction, the more its results will be able to receive the full complexity of social life.

For Lefebvre, the conventional understanding of the world as a collection of rigid oppositions, in which, for example, the *ideal* and the *real* must forever remain separate, deprives theory, research and practice of a powerful tool for drawing something new out of the given.

Elements of rhythmanalysis

The rhythms of greatest interest to Lefebvre are those that are observable in the everyday, not least because the everyday remains a reservoir of resistance to bureaucratised time. If the practice of rhythmanalysis is necessarily interdisciplinary, the figure of the rhythmanalytical practitioner must be so as well, such is the complexity of his or her objects of study:

Everywhere where there is interaction between a place, a time and an expenditure of energy, there is rhythm. [. . .] The rhythm analysis here defined as a method and a theory [. . .] [brings] together very different types of knowledge: medicine, history, climatology, cosmology, poetry (*the poetic*), etc. Not forgetting, of course, sociology and psychology. [. . .] The rhythmanalyst will have some points in common with the psychoanalyst. [. . .] He will be attentive. [. . .] He will listen to the world, and [. . .] to [. . .] noises, which are said without meaning, and to murmurs [. . .], full of meaning – and finally he will listen to silences. [. . .] He listens – and first to his body; he learns rhythm from it. [. . .] The rhythmanalyst calls on all his senses. He draws on his breathing, the circulation of his blood, the beatings of his heart and the delivery of his speech as landmarks. [. . .] He thinks with his body, not in the abstract, but in lived temporality. He does not neglect [. . .] smells, scents, the impressions that are so strong in the child and other living beings, which society atrophies. [. . .] He garbs himself in the tissue of the everyday. [. . .] He must simultaneously catch a rhythm and perceive it within the whole, in the same way as non-analysts, people, *perceive* it. He must arrive at the concrete through experience.

(Lefebvre 2004 [1992]: 15–16, 19, 21)

Elaborating further, Lefebvre intertwines method and practitioner as a function of the body, its senses and its rhythms. Beyond the attributes the rhythmanalyst must have, and the disciplines s/he must draw upon, or borrow from, the analyst's own body is his or her primary tool:

Just as he borrows and receives from his whole body and all his senses, so he receives data [. . .] from all the sciences. [. . .] In relation to the instruments with which specialists supply him, he pursues an interdisciplinary approach. Without omitting the spatial and places, of course, he makes himself more sensitive to times than to spaces. He will come to 'listen' to a house, a street, a town, as an audience listens to a symphony.

(Lefebvre 2004 [1992]: 22)

Arguably, architects' productions habitually betray human desires for what van Eyck called 'built homecoming', in which 'The Body. Our body. So neglected in philosophy' (and by architecture in its wake) is recollected (Lefebvre 2004 [1992]: 20; van Eyck 2008 [1961]; 2008 [1967]: 472). Accepting for a moment that architecture is half as wanting as portrayed here, the first question raised is whether this is inevitable. Indeed, as articulated by Ernst Bloch, Manfredo Tafuri and Fredric Jameson, architecture and the city would appear to be moribund. But do the rhythmanalyst's methods suggest ways of achieving a more sophisticated and amenable built environment? Or are architecture and urbanism so ensnared within the web of capitalist realism that they can embody only three narratives: the narrative of techno-science, including reductive functionalism; the narrative of space as commodity or product, the value of which turns on the degree to which it is exchangeable; and the narrative of excess value, in which architecture becomes luxury object (in whatever guise – avant-garde, mainstream or privileged)? Absent from each of these is architecture as *engaged*, in either the broadest social terms or with the relationship of the built environment to the human body as primary referent. And yet, if there is anything we can learn from Lefebvre, it is that the total systems presumed or professed across the full spectrum of politics or theory are not as complete as they appear. Even today, there are architects who recollect the body and rhythms in their work. For example, Swiss architect Peter Zumthor begins his design process with childlike wonder and a recollection of relevant 'bodily events'; the Thermal Baths (1993–1996) in Vals, Switzerland clearly shows the benefits of this method. (The Baths, it is worth noting, is owned by the municipality for the benefit also of the local community.) However, Zumthor's work is a significant exception to the mainstream of contemporary practice, rather than the rule.

The rhythmanalytical method holds out alternatives for architecture and urban practices by offering a comprehensive multidimensional approach to the problem of the constructed environment:

> **[R]hythmanalysis could change our perspective on surroundings because it changes our conception in relation to classical philosophy [Cartesianism in**

particular]. [. . .] The sensible, this scandal of philosophers from Plato to Hegel (re)takes primacy, transformed without magic (without metaphysics). Nothing inert in the *world*, [. . .] rhythms, slow or lively (in relation to us). (This garden that I have before my eyes appears differently to me now from a moment ago. [. . .])

(Lefebvre 2004 [1992]: 17)

Architects reawakened to the aliveness of the world by reinstating 'the sensible in consciousness and *thought*' might 'accomplish a tiny part of the *revolutionary* transformation of this world and this society in decline', not least by subverting the restrictions that the capitalist, neoliberal and globalising production of space imposes upon consciousness and the results of practice (Lefebvre 2004 [1992]: 26).

To achieve this, 'the rhythmanalyst concerns himself [or herself] with temporalities and their relations with wholes' (Lefebvre 2004 [1992]: 24). S/he links the *logical* and the *visceral*, and more so reclaims a place for the *vital body*, using a method that can analyse the repetitive, to potentially reveal *moments* of change and transformation. Rhythmanalysis outlines a method for gaining a broader understanding of the context within which projects are imagined. As a corrective to the unreality of so much architecture, it counters alienation in the built environment by *listening* to the actual places, people, settings and bodily habits or events – rhythms – around which work ought to be shaped (Lefebvre 2004 [1992]: 14).

The relativity of rhythms

Paradoxically, modes of architectural analysis, and their representation, tend to distance architects from the very variables that analysis is meant to bring closer to hand. The problem of translating data collected as part of project preliminaries is a stubborn one, so much so that site analysis and social mapping usually amount to little more than a series of unrevealing practice rituals; as quickly forgotten as embarked upon. It is precisely here that Lefebvre's multi-formed and many-pronged critique of architects' practices has its greatest resonance. Rhythmanalysis is but one suggestion of a partial corrective to architects' inevitably alienating practices (dominated by the visual and the abstract). Because most architects' mapping techniques are counterintuitively drawn from the social sciences, in particular from planning, they omit the 'spatial and places'; they also desensitise practitioners (and students) to the prime importance of *time* – even before a project has begun.

The regime of the capitalist city – made up of isolation and alienation, and dominated by spectacle and consumption – might seem inevitable, as certain as a law of nature, but Lefebvre asserts that the possible-impossible is only impossible in this moment of obscured possibility. Rhythmanalysis, with its emphasis on arriving at the concrete by way of the body, as a rhythmic instrument in tune with the rhythms of everyday life, suggests that the sorts of listening to the city that Lefebvre encourages not only propose a mode of resistance to the apparent inevitability of capitalist space and its city, but also articulate how close analysis can reveal those moments – of difference, or dissonance – out of which real change could emerge. The object of rhythmanalysis 'is neither the apparent, nor the phenomenal, but the present' and the rhythmanalyst's project is to reclaim 'the sensible', changing what s/he observes by setting 'it in motion' (Lefebvre 2004 [1992]: 22, 25). Observation of this sort is generative, or creative. The everyday – which is at the centre of Lefebvre's project – is simultaneously the rhythmanalyst's object of study and the locus of possibility.

Analysis of the everyday aims to identify those aspects of it that resist bureaucratic organisation by both state and private interests, to reveal it as a space of transformation. Accordingly, the rhythmanalyst's most radical gesture would be to 'fully' reinstate 'the sensible in consciousness and in *thought*', which would contribute to 'the *revolutionary* transformation of this world' (Lefebvre 2004 [1992]: 26). Most remarkably, Lefebvre believes that the rhythmanalyst can accomplish this without 'claiming to' have changed 'life', and without any 'declared political position'. Remaining un-implicated in this way ostensibly allows the rhythmanalyst a freer hand to contribute to the 'revolutionary transformation of' society (Lefebvre 2004 [1992]: 26). Lefebvre clearly sees the rhythmanalyst as being more than simply an observer, or an evenly hovering analyst; s/he actively engages, but also reflects, because 'in order to grasp the rhythms, a bit of time, a sort of meditation on time, the city, people is required' (Lefebvre 2004 [1992]: 26, 30).

Analysis of the everyday aims to identify those aspects of it that resist bureaucratic organisation by both state and private interests, to reveal it as a space of transformation. Accordingly, the rhythmanalyst's most radical gesture would be to 'fully' reinstate 'the sensible in consciousness and in *thought*'.

Rhythms are all those aspects of life lived that are graspable with the five senses: vision, hearing, smell, taste and touch. In order to understand a place, to have analysed it comprehensibly, the rhythmanalyst must be alive to all that is around him or her – to all the myriad rhythms, including duration: five senses and four dimensions. This sort of multidimensional analysis promises real benefits for architects. While completing a rhythmanalysis requires being alive to all of the rhythms encountered, the work is best conducted at a slight remove from the object of analysis:

> In order to grasp and analyse rhythms it is necessary to get outside them but not completely. [. . .] A certain exteriority enables the analytic intellect to function. However, to grasp rhythm it is necessary to have been *grasped* by it, one must *let oneself go*, give oneself over, abandon oneself to its duration. [. . .] [I]t is therefore necessary to situate oneself simultaneously inside and outside.
>
> (Lefebvre 2004 [1992]: 27)

Analysing rhythms is best done from the inside and outside of them simultaneously – both figuratively and literally – because, according to Lefebvre, 'exteriority enables the analytical intellect to function' (Lefebvre 2004 [1992]: 27). His conviction is that analysing rhythms makes them palpable, while concentrating attention on those aspects of life operating beyond the organisation of the 'omnipresent state', such that 'beyond the sensible and visible order, which reveals political power, other orders suggest themselves' (Lefebvre 2004 [1992]: 32). The suggestion of 'other orders' is simultaneously a precursor of the 'possible-impossible' and the utopian 'moment' of the everyday.

But if analysing the repetitive and mundane aspects of the everyday reveals a tacit utopianism, the standard procedures of development tend to turn on the primacy of two associated aspects of cities – just two – that are taken to represent the sum total of urban possibility in the present, at least from a real estate investment and development perspective. These two interrelated aspects conceive of the city as either *destination* or as *commerce*. *Destinations* are conceived of as places where *commercial exchange* occurs, or, at the very least, where it is made much easier. Commerce and destination have become almost interchangeable in the language of urban development: if *commerce* is not intensified by the creation of a *destination*, it will not be thought of as being the *highest and best use* of any land parcel. And because commercial exchange is always situated, even virtually, it requires a destination. Even a Web-based outlet such as Amazon is a 'real' destination (for commerce), despite not yet having (at the time of this writing) physical structures that shoppers can visit. By allowing destinations of and for consumption to become the primary aim of their work, architects are caught up in the extremely limited dominant conception of what makes cities vital. In concentrating on cyclical and linear rhythms that return focus to 'wandering the street', rhythmanalysis offers a way to potentially outmanoeuvre the regime of destinations and commerce, which reduces the urban environment to an extension of *leisure time*, while making it into the natural habitat of the *society of the spectacle* (characterised by overstimulation, distraction, boredom and alienation) (Lefebvre 2004 [1992]: 33). Wandering the streets and elevating them to the object of focus in cities, along with public spaces, immediately throws into question the creeping extension of mall space as the dominant architectural form and function.

Paris and the Mediterranean

'The cyclical is social organisation manifesting itself', according to Lefebvre, whereas, '[t]he linear is the daily grind, the routine, therefore the perpetual' (Lefebvre 2004 [1992]: 30). In Lefebvre's view, social organisation and chance are the province of traditional cities, in particular Mediterranean ones. To articulate the antithesis, Lefebvre singles out the Centre Georges Pompidou (1971–1977), on the Rue de Beaubourg, in Paris, for special attention. Designed by the Anglo-Italian partnership of Richard Rogers and Renzo Piano (with Irish engineer Peter Rice), who were known as exponents of so-called high-tech architecture, the Pompidou Centre was influenced by a range of techno-scientific achievements, including the 1960s accomplishments of NASA's (the US National Aeronautics and Space Administration) space programme, in particular the lunar module that landed on the moon in 1969, as well as by offshore oil drilling platforms, and the techno-utopianism of British architectural group Archigram (Coleman 2005: 65, 80–85). Amongst other spaces, the Pompidou includes a library, modern art museum, centre for modern music, bookstore, restaurant and cafes and vast public spaces, as well as the remarkable escalator that hangs off its front, rising upwards from just above the plaza to its summit offering expansive views of the city and access to the rooftop.

Lefebvre was preoccupied with the Pompidou Centre because of its location in the Marais, where he had lived for many years. It is a neighbourhood that has undergone dramatic changes during the post–World War II years, not least by being, as Lefebvre observed, 'Americanised', including the addition of a shopping mall, fast food restaurants, chain store shopping and the Pompidou, which ironically could appear to be a building and an institution – a cultural centre – right in line with Lefebvre's thinking, not least for the expansive urban concrete *beach* that extends from its entrance on an incline to Rue Saint-Martin. Moreover, its interior organisation was planned as infinitely flexible, open to all sorts of unanticipated uses and forms of occupation (though this has been more difficult to achieve than planned in the galleries and public spaces of the building). Although the interior of the Pompidou could be construed as its *content*, it is best known for its exterior, which, on a socio-cultural level, may have more significance than the functions within. The Pompidou is an exoskeleton that inverts usual expectation by exposing the building's structure and services as a kind of modern-day decorative representation (rather than hiding them within). Moreover, by displaying the building's structure – its bones and supports – for all to see, the building appears undressed, naked, further emphasising its radical rethinking of culture and propriety.

Interestingly, although the Pompidou appears an ecstatic celebration of machine production, it has a strangely handmade quality, as a one-off, rather than the result of mass production, even at the level of individual elements, which surprisingly embody a reassuring humanness both in the quality of manufacture and in the scale of these parts fitted together to form an almost overwhelming whole, at the scales of the human body, the neighbourhood in which it sits and the traditional city it begins to fragment (but also paradoxically unifies).

As an *architecture of the event*, ostensibly open to all sorts of unanticipated and improvised uses, one might imagine that Lefebvre ought to have lavished high praise on the Pompidou Centre. As it turns out, this was not the case, and understanding why illuminates what Lefebvre lamented in the modern city, as well as what he hoped for. Interestingly, Lefebvre does not identify the Pompidou Centre by name, but his allusions are unmistakable. If the traditional city and rhythms begin with the body – '[t]he windows, doors, streets and facades are measured in proportion to human size [. . .] [t]he little bistros on *Rue R.*, are on a human scale, like the passers by' – the Pompidou Centre appears to overpower such familiar conceptions of scale (Lefebvre 2004 [1992]: 33):

> **Opposite, the constructions wanted to *transcend* this scale, to leave known dimensions and also all models known and possible behind; leading to the exhibition of metal and frozen guts, in the form of solidified piping, and the harshest reflections. And it is a meteorite from another planet, where technocracy reigns untrammelled.**
>
> **(Lefebvre 2004 [1992]: 33, 34)**

Centre Georges Pompidou, Paris, France, Studio Piano & Rogers, Architects (1971–1977)

Rather than being impressed with its novelty, or heresy, Lefebvre observes something as alien as it is alienating. A grotesque construction that, at least for him, contributed to the gutting of a neighbourhood – and its rhythms – he knew intimately. But, much as architects might attempt to hide behind the apparent social or political neutrality of *aesthetic* concerns, Lefebvre is well aware that something else is at play, more so than even the banal claims for the arts-and commerce-led regeneration of an aging inner-city quarter.

'What', he asked, 'does the proximity between a certain archaism attached to history and the exhibited supra-modernity whisper?' Discerning or decoding this is a crucial aspect of the architect's work that is rarely considered, which is why what is designed is often a remarkably naïve carrier of meanings all but invisible to the author of a work. Lefebvre continues by wondering: 'Does the state political order write across this scene [. . .]? Without doubt'. Not surprisingly, he identifies money as the 'determining factor'. 'But' in our epoch, 'money no longer renders itself sensible as such, even on the façade of the bank. The centre of Paris bears the imprint of what it hides, but it hides it' (Lefebvre 2004 [1992]: 34). In no small way, colonisation of the centre of the city by money and its interests, in collaboration with the state political order, extends the foreclosure of the 'right to the city' with almost every new development project. What is lost, Lefebvre laments, is the passing of 'something of the provincial, of the medieval: historic and crumbling' that until '[n]ot long ago' the *capital* centre of Paris retained' (Lefebvre 2004 [1992]: 34).

In no small way, colonisation of the centre of the city by money and its interests, in collaboration with the state political order, extends the foreclosure of the 'right to the city' with almost every new development project.

Continuing, Lefebvre expands his description of what is lost: 'First, the spectacle of the junction and the perpendicular street which, not long ago, formed a neighbourhood of the city, peopled by a sort of native, with many artisans and small shopkeepers. In short, people of the neighbourhood. [. . .] Production has left these places' (Lefebvre 2004 [1992]: 35). Perhaps recognising his drift towards morbid nostalgia for things past, Lefebvre shifts to a more conciliatory tone, observing in the crowds now populating both older and more modern squares something of a resurgence: 'it would be too easy to say that it has lost its innocence. The squares have re-found their ancient function, for a long time imperilled, of gathering, of setting the scene and staging spontaneous popular theatre' (Lefebvre 2004 [1992]: 35). Nevertheless, a degree of ambivalence shows through:

> Here on the square between Saint-Merri and Modernism erupts a medieval-looking festival: fire eaters, jugglers, snake charmers, but also preachers and sit-in discussions. Openness and discussion next to dogmatic

armour-plating. All possible games, material and spiritual. [. . .] They almost never stop, eating some hot-dog or other as they walk (rapid Americanisation). [. . .] Watching, half-listening to those pitching their wares, then taking up again their unrelenting march. [. . .] There on the square, there is something maritime about the rhythms. Currents traverse the masses. Streams break off, which bring or take away participants. Some of them go towards the jaws of the monster [the Pompidou Centre], which gobbles them down in order quite quickly to throw them back up. [. . .] With these places are we in the everyday? Well, the one doesn't prevent the other and the pseudo-fête emerges only apparently from the everyday.

(Lefebvre 2004 [1992]: 35–36)

The 'pseudo-fête' of entertainment cities, of spectacle, is revealed as the province of some perpetual big night out, in which the apparent exuberance of the celebration thinly veils its disconnection from everyday rhythms, and its capture within the domain of consumption; a condition summed up by Lefebvre as: 'At the end of the week, in place of the traditional day of rest and piety, "Saturday Night Fever" breaks out' (Lefebvre and Régulier 2004 [1985]: 74).

If Lefebvre is discouraged by cities shaped in the image of capital, or, more accurately deformed by it, he discovers in Mediterranean cities urban social forms robust and wily enough to resist most forms of central control and (re)development which have as their objective transformation of the *qualitative* – social and urban forms of the pre-modern, pre-industrial city – into the *quantitative*, overly organised, centrally planned cities of modern architecture. In Lefebvre's terms, the shift from traditional city to fragmented city parallels the shift from pre-industrial labour to its division and, in particular, the adoption of the decimal system's powers of ten at the expense of the duodecimal system. The latter relate to 'cyclical repetitions' whereas the former relate to 'linear repetitions'; the latter suggest 'rotations', whereas the former suggest 'trajectories'. Cyclical repetitions are 'generally cosmic in origin'; consisting of the cyclical, rhythms of days, nights, months, and 'the seasons and years. And tides!' The cyclical analogises the 360 degrees of a circle, and thus the planet earth as well. The base twelve system encompasses 'the twelve hours of the clock-face [. . .] the twelve signs of the zodiac and even a dozen eggs or oysters, which means to say that the measure of twelve extends itself to living matter in direct provenance from nature' (Lefebvre and Régulier 2004 [1986]: 90). It is not so much that an architect working in base twelve, as opposed to base ten, will necessarily produce more humane environments, but rather that the decimal system is fully implicated in the industrial production processes that have fragmented the city.

For Lefebvre, '[c]yclical rhythms [. . .] are also the rhythms of beginning again: of the "returning". [. . .] The dawn is always new. The linear, by contrast, defines itself through the consecution and reproduction of the same phenomenon, almost identical, if not identical' (Lefebvre and Régulier 2004 [1986]: 90). Although he appears to oppose the linear and the cyclical here, Lefebvre's real objective is to highlight their qualitative difference. So, even if the cyclical of the duodecimal system is the rhythm of 'beginning again' and the linear of the decimal, or metric, system 'is the point of departure for all that is mechanical', Lefebvre is clear that 'the analysis that separated them must join them back together because they enter into perpetual interaction and are even relative to one another, to the extent that one serves as the measure of the other' (Lefebvre and Régulier 2004 [1986]: 90). As an example, Lefebvre offers up 'so many days of work': days being cyclical and rhythmic, whereas work is linear (Lefebvre and Régulier 2004 [1986]: 90).

Metric organisation of human and social activities, and imposition of the decimal system by a centralising state on the body-centric rhythms of the everyday, transforms urban space and social life alike. However, for Lefebvre, as noted earlier, Mediterranean cities model a setting in which the right to the city can be achieved, and has been. Yet, as Cartesian notions of space (which are both abstract and absolute) – especially modern fragmented additions to historic centres – encroach upon Mediterranean cities, the spaces of resistance, of difference, and the multiple rhythms that long characterised these cities are diminished. In Lefebvre's terms, this makes them less Mediterranean and more Nordic; less solar and more lunar, and, at least apparently, more dominated by centralised control (Lefebvre and Régulier 2004 [1986]: 91–92). In solar towns 'one can expect [. . .] a more intense life than in lunar towns, but also one richer in contrasts at the very heart of the town' (Lefebvre and Régulier 2004 [1986]: 92).

According to Lefebvre, public spaces and the layout of towns, inflected by dynamic topography, are key features of Mediterranean cities and the rhythms that characterise them. In modern cities, public space and topography are typically either diminished or obliterated; and where topography is allowed to stand, it tends to be mastered by technique. And where public space is allowed to flourish, it tends to be consumed, transformed into a stage of consumption rather than of sociability or political action. In this regard, Lefebvre asserts that in Mediterranean towns, 'urban, which is to say public, space becomes the site of a vast staging where all these [social and intimate] relations with their rhythms show and unfurl themselves. Rites, codes and relations make themselves visible here: they act themselves out here' (Lefebvre and Régulier 2004 [1986]: 96). As such, the Mediterranean city persists for Lefebvre as a model of urbanism that runs counter to almost all contemporary urban practices implicated in (re)shaping of cities since at least the nineteenth century. In recollecting Mediterranean towns, Lefebvre was not encouraging a nostalgic redeployment of the past in the present. Rather, as was suggested earlier, looking backwards is the source of his radical critique of the present, and the roots of his project for different kinds of spaces in the city.

Lefebvre asserts that in Mediterranean towns, 'urban, which is to say public, space becomes the site of a vast staging where all these [social and intimate] relations with their rhythms show and unfurl themselves'.

While Lefebvre's admiration for Mediterranean towns does not become a blueprint for action, their peculiar rhythms have much to tell us: 'All forms of hegemony and homogeneity are refused in the Mediterranean. [. . .] [I]t is the very idea of centrality that is refused, because each group [. . .] considers itself the centre. [. . .] The polyrhythmia of Mediterranean towns highlights their common character through their differences' (Lefebvre and Régulier 2004 [1986]: 98). Yet, even if the lived intensity of Mediterranean cities may not be transferable, reflecting on them can inform more sophisticated practices. In a consideration of still existing public space established in pre-modern Venice, Lefebvre observes a particular urban rhythm at play that required the specificity of that space to appear:

> Isn't Venice a theatrical city [. . .], where the audience [. . .] and the actors are the same [. . .]? Thus we imagine the Venice of Casanova, of Visconti's *Senso*, like the Venice of today. Isn't that because a privileged form of civility, of liberty, founded on and in a dialectic of rhythms, gives itself free rein in this space? This liberty does not consist in the fact of being a free citizen within the state – but being free in the city outside the state. [. . .] Through a certain use of time the citizen resists the state. [. . .] Thus public space, the space of representation, becomes 'spontaneously' a place for walks and encounters, intrigues, diplomacy, ideals and negotiations – it theatralises itself.
>
> **(Lefebvre and Régulier 2004 [1986]: 96)**

Reflecting on the enduring qualities of Venice (and Mediterranean cities), rationality and progress do not provide adequate explanations for the general regularisation of modern cities, which includes eradication of spaces of subversion and dissent. Instead, control quickly emerges as a more convincing explanation.

In terms of topography, Lefebvre observes 'right around the Mediterranean a remarkable architecture of the stairway'. If stairways form '[a] link between spaces' they 'also' ensure 'a link between the time of architecture (the house, the enclosure) and urban time (the street, the open space, the square and the monuments)' (Lefebvre and Régulier 2004 [1986]: 97). Lefebvre asks: 'Now is the stairway not a localised time *par excellence*?' For example '[d]on't the steps in Venice', as elsewhere in the Mediterranean, 'rhythm the walk through the city, while serving simultaneously as a transition between different rhythms'? (Lefebvre and Régulier 2004 [1986]: 97). Steps can also be a more 'initiatory [. . .] passage' into a city than even a 'gate or an avenue', depending on their 'monumentality', and because they impose 'on the body and on consciousness the requirement of passing from one rhythm to another, as yet unknown – to be discovered' (Lefebvre and Régulier 2004 [1986]: 97). To appreciate the veracity of this, one need only reflect on any condition familiar to him or her where either a stair has been removed (even a very short run) and replaced with a regularised or smoothed over pathway to encourage smooth flows of movement, or, less likely, the rhythmic difference where a notable exterior urban stair has been constructed. The demands stairs make on the body, in terms of physical activity and concentration, encourages a mindfulness that renders the location present, while inflecting both its rhythms and the body's own.

In his oscillation between pessimism, or potentially morbid nostalgia, and genuine optimism, which is in turn counterbalanced by a degree of ambivalence, Lefebvre models a way of thinking through the changes imposed on cities cognizant of the real dangers of adopting transformations in the name of *progress*, modernity, novelty or efficiency. Obviously, not all change is good, and not all aesthetic, economic or development fashions promise improvements, or even benefits. Imposing redevelopments without thinking them through in as multidimensional a manner as possible risks achieving discouraging results that must be lived with for a lifetime or longer. The desire of architects, money and power to make their imprint on a city begs for considered analysis and thoughtful doubt. A more balanced mental attitude able to perceive the rhythms of the city 'requires', as Lefebvre observes, 'equally attentive eyes and ears, a head and a heart. A memory? Yes in order to grasp the present otherwise than in an instantaneous moment, to restore it in its moments, in the movements of diverse rhythms. The recollection of other moments and of all hours is indispensable' (Lefebvre 2004 [1992]: 36). While suggesting a particular kind of attitude towards *listening to the city* to apprehend its rhythms, this approach also has implications for the way architects collect and represent data and communicate designs: 'No camera, no image or series of images can show these rhythms' (Lefebvre 2004 [1992]: 36).

The perils of capital

As a caution also relevant to architects, Lefebvre alerts us to the fact that 'Capital kills social richness' even as it 'produces *private* riches, just as it pushes the private individual to the fore, despite it being a public monster. It increases political struggle to the extent that states and state-apparatuses bow down to it' (Lefebvre 2004 [1992]: 53–54). Although architects might prefer to imagine themselves, or so-called aesthetic concerns, as being immune to the corrosive influence of capital, Lefebvre observes that 'Architecture and the architect threatened with disappearance capitulate before the *property developer*, who spends the money'. In tandem with this condition, 'pre-capitalist architecture [and] communal [. . .] forms of social life have been ruined on a world scale. Without replacement, except by a gestating *socialism*' (Lefebvre 2004 [1992]: 54). In an attempt to articulate a sense of what has been lost, Lefebvre outlines the spatial correlate of 'social richness' that 'dates from an earlier time', characterised by 'parks, squares and avenues, open monumentality, etc.'. However, in our epoch, '[i]nvestment in this domain [. . .] grows rarer', or is privatised (transformed from a public benefit into a private luxury) (Lefebvre 2004 [1992]: 54).

According to Lefebvre, in place of social richness, empty cages are set up, 'which can receive any commodity whatsoever', places 'of transit, of passage, where the crowds contemplate themselves (example: the Beaubourg Centre – the Forum [shopping mall] in Paris – the [World] Trade Centre in New York)' (Lefebvre 2004 [1992]: 54). In his view, capital 'constructs and erects itself on a contempt for life and its foundation: the body, the time of living'. The disdain capital has for life 'makes up for itself with ornaments; refinements in hygiene, the proliferation of sports and sporting ideology' (Lefebvre 2004 [1992]: 52). Architecture is so difficult in the hollow space of capital precisely because 'Capital does not construct. It produces. It does not edify; it reproduces itself. It simulates life. Production and re-production tend to coincide in the uniform. [. . .] [Capital] kills nature. It kills the town. [. . .] It kills artistic creation, creative capacity. [. . .] It dislocates humans' (Lefebvre 2004 [1992]: 53).

Despite this bleak outlook, earlier I described Lefebvre as a philosopher of cracks, in the sense that he is convinced that although the everyday – characterised by the mundane, or banal, and the repetitive – might appear as a closed system out of which innovation or change cannot possibly emerge, in fact, it harbours real, albeit as yet undiscovered, possibilities. Routine seems to preclude transformation by disciplining the body (as an individual and social being alike) to the demands of regimentation, bureaucratisation and so-called human resource management. But it is precisely the apparent certainties of control – of standardised patterns of behaviour – that mask possibility. Innovations can emerge out of the repetitive; even though 'Humans are [apparently] broken-in through repetition'. Whereas simple rewards suffice for animals in assuring this process, humans *ritualise* otherwise mechanical repetition. Lefebvre uses the word *dressage* for this process, which is the act of taming, training or breaking an animal; whereby complex movements are committed to memory and recalled on command. According to Lefebvre, *dressage* is localised in space and time: changing across cultures, and within a given culture through time. As such, 'gestures cannot be attributed to nature' (Lefebvre 2004 [1992]: 38–39).

Routine seems to preclude transformation by disciplining the body (as an individual and social being alike) to the demands of regimentation, bureaucratisation and so-called human resource management.

Dressage, or training, establishes a rhythm that is internalised through repetition, such that the aims it achieves are accepted as more natural than habits, and are not questioned. Organised education from the earliest age surely plays a role in assuring conformity through socialisation, but so does professional education, including in architecture. While it might seem obvious and necessary that a certain degree of conformity is internalised in order to function within a society or a profession, left unexamined, achievement of this quickly forecloses on alternative ways of imagining, thinking or doing. Automatic as socialised responses and behaviours can seem, the internalisation of such standardisation is never as uniform as might be desired. It is precisely this inescapable irregularity, even within the most apparently regular of systems that opens up opportunities: 'All becoming irregular [. . .] of rhythms produces antagonistic effects. It *throws out of order* and disrupts. [. . .] It can also produce a lacuna, a hole in time, to be filled in by an invention, a creation. [. . .] Disruptions and crises always have origins in and effects on rhythms' (Lefebvre 2004 [1992]: 44).

Paradoxically, then, invention can emerge, in fact is only possible, when rhythms are disrupted. On closer consideration, however, although invention may only emerge out of crises, it still requires the backdrop of relatively stable rhythms. Thought of in this way, one of the key reasons for engaging in a rhythmanalysis would be to identify both the rhythms according to which given conditions flow along, but also to begin identifying a potential crisis point, or points of potential disruption, or holes in time (the cracks introduced earlier), that could be widened to include invention. Rhythms, like the everyday, have a double character: both are simultaneously arbiters of conformity *and* possible grounds of radical transformation.

Colonisation of the everyday by the desacralized clockwork time of capital threatens to subjugate all other aspects of life to work. And yet the everyday is concurrently 'shot through and traversed' by what Lefebvre calls 'great cosmic and vital rhythms' which include 'day and night, the months and the seasons, and [. . .] biological rhythms' (Lefebvre and Régulier 2004 [1985]: 73). He characterises these opposing modes of time as the 'linear' – made up of 'brutal repetitions' that are 'tiring, exhausting and tedious', and the 'cyclical' – having 'the appearance of an event and an advent', which makes it also the province of the rhythmic (Lefebvre and Régulier 2004 [1985]: 73). Expanding on this, Lefebvre states that 'only a non mechanical movement can have rhythm: this classes everything that emerges [. . .] from the purely mechanical in the domain of the quantitative; abstractly detached from quality', whereas '[r]hythm [. . .] brings with it a differentiated time, a qualified duration' (Lefebvre and Régulier

2004 [1985]: 78). The opposite is 'the quantified time of watches and clocks [that imposes] monotonous repetitions' (Lefebvre and Régulier 2004 [1985]: 76).

The rhythmanalyst and the architect

For Lefebvre, rhythm is space-time, emphasising the interdependence of the temporal and the spatial as a challenge to the conventional dichotomising of the two concepts. Rhythm is also the occupation, or inflection, of space in time. As such, rhythm introduces the fourth dimension of time to three-dimensional spatial conceptions. In turn, the association of space with time localises time by relating it to specific conditions. Four-dimensional thinking raises a significant challenge to the predominance of limited three-dimensional (or even two-dimensional) conceptualisations of architecture. In this regard, van Eyck, for example, attempted to socialise space-time to make an interdependent conception of both concepts relevant to architecture. He renders specific the abstractness of space – as infinitely extensible, and isotropic – and the generality of time – as either repetitive, or linear – by recasting them as 'place and occasion', which localises both, even if neither is ever permanently fixed. A further intersection between van Eyck and Lefebvre is evident in their shared understanding of the relation of space to time (and vice versa) as *relative*, rather than *absolute*. The occupation of cities and buildings is always rhythmic or polyrhythmic, in the sense that even habitual inhabitation is in each instance a form of re-inhabitation that is rather more fluid (rhythmical) than fixed (mechanistic, or repetitive). Accordingly, Lefebvre asserted that 'concrete times have rhythms, or rather are rhythms – and all rhythms imply the relation of a time to a space, a localised time, or if one prefers, a temporalized space. Rhythm is always linked to such and such a place. [. . .] Let us insist on the relativity of rhythms. [. . .] A rhythm is only slow or fast in relation to other rhythms with which it finds itself associated in a more or less vast unity', constituting an *open*, rather than a *closed* totality (Lefebvre and Régulier 2004 [1986]: 89).

The coupling of space and time in architecture offers much more than the sort of modern dynamism suggested by Sigfried Giedion in *Space, Time and Architecture*, or the exhilarating drama of Le Corbusier's *promenade architecturale*, which has the tendency of putting a building on display as an object above all else, admittedly as one moves through it. Lefebvre's coupling of 'space-time', analogously stated as 'place and occasion' by van Eyck, and recollected as 'habits' or 'improvised use', and the emphasis on 'bodily event' by Zumthor demonstrates how Lefebvre's preoccupation with 'rhythm and rhythmanalysis' could contribute to revaluing architecture's social vocation, and with it the centrality of the human body to this. Recuperating the human body as simultaneously subject, object and model for social structuring and restructuring, and the architecture and cities that shelter, or instigate, such possibilities, improves the chances of realising a more humane constructed environment. Lefebvre's emphasis on rhythm and the possibility of a rhythmanalysis is mirrored in van Eyck's associated conception of relativity and 'right size' (Coleman 2005: 200–213).

Anticipating the reservations he imagined some readers would have with the rhythmanalytical project, Lefebvre emphasised the value of working across

Municipal Baths, Vals, Switzerland, Peter Zumthor (completed 1996)

disciplines: 'The rhythmanalytical project applied to the urban can seem disparate, because it appeals to, in order to bring together, notions and aspects that analysis too often keeps separate: time and space, the public and the private, the state-political and the intimate' (Lefebvre and Régulier 2004 [1986]: 100). Importantly, this would be an advance in knowledge precisely because it associates time and space, which Lefebvre argues most branches of knowledge have traditionally separated 'as two entities or two clearly distinct substances'. More specifically, according to Lefebvre, 'we continue to divide up time into lived time, measured time, historical time, work time, and free time, everyday time, etc., that are most often studied outside of their spatial context' (Lefebvre and Régulier 2004 [1986]: 89). So, in addition to conceptualising space and time as associated, the rhythmanalytical project asserts the importance of spatial considerations in the understanding of social life. By the same token, although 'contemporary theories [. . .] show a relation between time and space, or more exactly [. . .] how they are relative to one another', as such, rhythmanalysis counters the continuing habit of dividing them (Lefebvre and Régulier 2004 [1986]: 89).

So, in addition to conceptualising space and time as associated, the rhythmanalytical project asserts the importance of spatial considerations in the understanding of social life.

Conceptualising space and time as relational encourages analyses that are comparative rather than *a priori*, or absolute in character. 'Relativist thought' according to Lefebvre, 'obliges us to reject all definitive and fixed references', such that any 'frame of reference can only be provisional or conjunctural' (Lefebvre and Régulier 2004 [1985]: 83). More concretely, if space and time are relative, they are also situational, which means they can shift according to changing conditions. In this sense, it becomes impossible to think about space (place, architecture, the city) as separate from the conditions within which it is produced. The impossibility of an autonomous architecture is thus asserted implicitly. By the same token, the necessity of rethinking Utopia as dialectical emerges, in a way that anticipates geographer David Harvey's proposition in *Spaces of Hope* that utopias of *spatial closure*, of architecture and urban projects, which tend towards the authoritarian, are counterbalanced by the open-endedness of utopias of *social process*, which tend towards indeterminateness in their avoidance of closure. For Harvey, who clearly follows Lefebvre, a dialectical utopianism assures a 'stronger utopianism' that 'integrates social process and spatial form' in a 'spatiotemporal utopianism – a dialectical utopianism – rooted in our present possibilities at the same time as it points toward different trajectories for human uneven geographical developments' (Harvey 2000: 196).

By setting as one of his or her objectives 'separating as little as possible the scientific from the poetic' the rhythmanalyst can begin thinking the spatial and temporal together, as noted, by drawing upon multiple disciplines, including psychology, sociology and anthropology, amongst others (Lefebvre and Régulier 2004 [1986]: 87). Working in this way makes it possible for rhythmanalysts to 'listen to a house, a street, a town, as one listens to a symphony, an opera. [. . .] The rhythmanalyst thus knows how to listen to a square, a market, an avenue' (Lefebvre and Régulier 2004 [1986]: 87, 89). As part of his or her work, the rhythmanalyst 'seeks to know how this music is composed, who plays it and for whom' (Lefebvre and Régulier 2004 [1986]: 87). Equally, the rhythmanalyst 'has the duty of remaining attentive [. . .] to the relativity of rhythms' (Lefebvre and Régulier 2004 [1985]: 91).

CHAPTER 5

Conclusion

Another scale?

> Analysis and knowledge presuppose concepts (categories), but also a point
> of departure (enabling us to compose and enumerate a scale). We know
> that a rhythm is slow or lively only in relation to other rhythms (often our
> own: those of our walking, our breathing, our heart). This is the case even
> though each rhythm has its own and specific measure: speed, frequency,
> consistency. Spontaneously, each of us has our preferences, references, fre-
> quencies; each must appreciate rhythms by referring them to oneself, one's
> heart or breathing, but also to one's hours of work, of rest, of waking and
> of sleep.
>
> (Lefebvre 2004 [1992]: 10)

My attempt throughout this book has been threefold: to introduce Lefebvre's
thought on space, everyday life, Utopia and cities to architects and others
occupied with inventing and constructing architecture and the city; to help
Lefebvre speak directly to those same individuals in an intelligible way;
and finally to reveal the continuing relevance of Lefebvre's thought for the
theory and practice of architecture, and cognate disciplines, in the present. If
in any way successful, this slim book will ideally make some small contribution
to encouraging architects to think their own thoughts; and to begin doing
so by reflecting on the habits, practices and omissions that characterise
their own discipline, which are all too often taken for granted or accepted
as given.

If Lefebvre teaches us anything, it is to recognise, in any apparent certainty
taken as a fully closed totality, an expression of hubris; but more so, to recognise
an opportunity for subversion. Wherever the overconfidence of apparent
inevitabilities may be asserted, a crack will surely appear that can be widened,
however slowly, until the light of other possibilities shines through. What might

have seemed impossible only moments ago could ultimately emerge as actually possible. No form of optimism could be of greater value to architects.

However, in doing something with Lefebvre – thinking with him, or inviting him to encourage us to think our own thoughts – it is worth remembering that he never lost sight either of the body or of the inheritance of the past, even when imagining a radically different future. Lefebvre's quarrel was not with civilisation or with tradition, but rather with the deformities wrought by capital in the modern techno-scientific age. Whatever else, the centrality of the body in his project is paramount:

> Man (the species): his physical and physiological being is indeed the measure of the world, as in the ancient dictum of Protagoras. It is not only that our knowledge is relative to our constitution, but rather that the world that offers itself up to us (nature, the earth and what we call the sky, the body and its insertion in social relations) is relative to this constitution. Not to *a priori* categories, but to our senses and the instruments we have at our disposal. More philosophically: another scale would determine another world. Same? Without doubt but differently grasped.
>
> (Lefebvre and Régulier 2004 [1985] : 83)

However, in doing something with Lefebvre – thinking with him, or inviting him to encourage us to think our own thoughts – it is worth remembering that he never lost sight either of the body or of the inheritance of the past, even when imagining a radically different future.

In an age of increasing virtuality, the idea that human beings are the measure of all things, in the sense that all that is out there and all that is made is

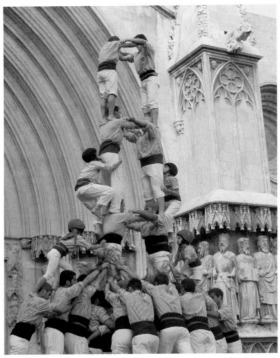

'Building Community: Human Tower' (training for the *Concurs de Castells de Tarragona*), Tarragona, Spain (July 2012)

understood by way of reference to the human frame, could seem archaic at best. But architects forget the continuity of the human form at their peril. Obviously, recollecting this does not preclude invention, but rather situates it, as Lefebvre asserts:

> [T]he human species draws from the heart of the universe movements that correspond to its own movements. [. . .] What is fashioned, formed and produced is established on this scale. [. . .] This is the scale of the earth, of accidents on the earth's surface and the cycles that unfurl there. [. . .] What is created does not refer back to this scale, it either exceeds or transfigures it.
>
> (Lefebvre and Régulier 2004 [1985]: 83)

Thus, although the scale of the body is in constant dialogue with the scale of the world, Lefebvre anticipates that this scale will either be exceeded or transfigured. However, rather than being an exclusively either/or condition, we will arguably only ever be able to surpass this tension in our works when we have successfully transformed it, in particular by making our world a better home for the social and intimate rhythms of everyday life.

Further reading

Although Lefebvre's influence on thinking in architecture is undeniable, as architectural theorist K. Michael Hays observes, 'his program has not been fully developed in architecture theory' (Hays 2000: 175); thus, although this book is meant to be something of a corrective, there is not much writing from within architecture that deals directly with Lefebvre. Consequently, the best place to go for further reading is Lefebvre himself. Although not all of his writing has been translated into English, many of the more than sixty books he wrote have been. An obvious place to begin one's further reading of Lefebvre is with the books that figure most prominently in this study, *The Production of Space* and *Rhythmanalysis*. After those two books, *The Right to the City* and *Critique of Everyday Life* (3 volumes) are good places to go. See also the recently translated first publication of Lefebvre's *Toward and Architecture of Enjoyment* (2014), originally written between 1973 and 1974.

Coming from within the architecture discipline, the architectural historian and theorist closest in spirit to Lefebvre (albeit coincidentally) is Joseph Rykwert. Although Lefebvre appears to make no mention of Rykwert in his writing, Rykwert does mention Lefebvre at least once (2002 [2000]: 265, n. 5). Nevertheless, if this present study sparks an interest in Lefebvre that in turn inspires a desire to rethink architecture in a social register, the avid reader is encouraged to consider the correspondences between Lefebvre and Rykwert evident in Rykwert's writing from *The Idea of a Town: The Anthropology of Urban Form in Rome, Italy, and the Ancient World* (first published in 1963) to *The Seduction of Place: The History and Future of Cities* (first published in 2000), and conversely in Lefebvre's *The Production of Space*.

As suggested in the introduction to this book, Dutch architect Aldo van Eyck worked in an arguably Lefebvrian manner, and as such provides examples, in both his writing and built work, of practices echoing many of Lefebvre's concerns. See for example, his *Works* for an introduction to his architecture, and *Writings* for an exhaustive compilation of his writings. For more on van Eyck, see also my own *Utopias and Architecture*.

For a more explicit discussion on Lefebvre's association with architects and architecture, see Lukasz Stanek's recent *Henri Lefebvre on Space: Architecture, Urban Research, and the Production of Theory*. Along these same lines, see *Autogestion, or Henri Lefebvre in New Belgrade*, which includes a text by Lefebvre that was submitted along with a proposal by French architects with whom he was collaborating on an entry to the International Competition for the New Belgrade Urban Structure Improvement in 1986, sponsored by the former Yugoslavian state.

For an introduction to how Lefebvre's ideas have taken shape in the work of other thinkers, see geographer David Harvey's *Rebel Cities* and *Spaces of Hope*. A final book worth examining is *Architecture of the Everyday*, edited by architects Deborah Berke and Steven Harris, who teach design at Yale University. The book is an intriguing attempt, in a wide variety of essays by a range of authors, to shift Lefebvre's preoccupation with the *everyday* into an explicit consideration of its relevance for architectural theory and practice.

Bibliography

Augé, M. (1995) *Non-Places, Introduction to an Anthropology of Supermodernity*, trans. John Howe, London: Verso.

Berke, D. and Harris, S., Eds. (1997) *Architecture of the Everyday*, New York: Princeton Architectural Press.

Bitter, S., Weber, H. and Derksen, J., Eds. (2009) *Autogestion: Or Henri Lefebvre in New Belgrade*, Berlin: Sternberg Press. Includes a facsimile of an unpublished text by Lefebvre accompanying a competition entry for the design of a New Belgrade.

Bloch, E. (1959) 'Building in Empty Spaces', reprinted in *The Utopian Function of Art and Literature: Selected Essays* (1988), trans. Jack Zipes and Frank Mecklenburg, Cambridge, MA: MIT Press.

Boersma, L. (2005) 'Constant' (Interview with Constant), *BOMB* 91 (spring), ART, available online at: http://bombsite.com/issues/91/articles/2713 [Accessed 30 August 2013].

Coleman, A. (1985) *Utopia on Trial*, London: Hilary Shipman.

Coleman, N. (2014) 'Architecture and Dissidence: Utopia as Method', *Architecture and Culture*, vol. 2, no. 1 March, pp. 45–60.

Coleman, N. (2013a) ' "Building in Empty Spaces": Is Architecture a "Degenerate Utopia"?', *Journal of Architecture*, vol. 18, no. 2 April, pp. 135–166.

Coleman, N. (2013b) 'Recovering Utopia', *Journal of Architecture Education*, vol. 67, no. 1 March, pp. 24–26.

Coleman, N. (2013c) 'Utopian Prospect of Henri Lefebvre', *Space and Culture*, vol. 16, no. 3 August, pp. 349–363.

Coleman, N. (2012a) 'Utopia and Modern Architecture?', *Architectural Research Quarterly*, vol. 16, no. 4 December, pp. 339–348.

Coleman, N. (2012b) 'Utopic Pedagogies: Alternatives to Degenerate Architecture', *Utopian Studies*, vol. 23, no. 2 December, pp. 314–354.

Coleman, N., Ed. (2011) *Imagining & Making the World: Reconsidering Architecture & Utopia*, Oxford: Peter Lang.

Coleman, N. (2008) 'Elusive Interpretations', *Cloud-Cuckoo-Land, International Journal of Architectural Theory*, Special Issue on the Interpretation of Architecture (1), Theory of Interpretation, vol. 12, no. 2 December 2008, available online at: http://www.cloud-cuckoo.net/journal1996-2013/inhalt/en/issue/issues/207/Coleman/coleman.php [Accessed 14 November 2014].

Coleman, N. (2007) 'Building Dystopia', *Rivista MORUS – Utopia e Renascimento* (Brasile), no. 4, pp. 181–192.

Coleman, N. (2005) *Utopias and Architecture*, Abingdon, Oxon: Routledge.

Daniel, J. O. and Moylan, T., Eds. (1997), *Not Yet, Reconsidering Ernst Bloch*, London: Verso.

Elden, S. (2001) 'Politics, Philosophy, Geography: Henri Lefebvre in Recent Anglo-American Scholarship', *Antipode*, vol. 33, no. 5 November, pp. 809–825.

Fisher, M. (2009) *Capitalist Realism: Is There No Alternative?*, Ropley, Hants: O Books.

Frampton, K. (1980/2007) *Modern Architecture: A Critical History*, 4th revised edition, London: Thames and Hudson Ltd.

Gardiner, M. E. (2004) 'Everyday Utopianism, Lefebvre and His Critics', *Cultural Studies*, vol. 18, no. 2/3 March/May, pp. 228–254.

Giedion, S. *Space, Time and Architecture. The Growth of a New Tradition* (1948), Fifth Edition, Revised and Enlarged (1966, 1982), Cambridge, MA: Harvard University Press.

Harvey, D. (2012) *Rebel Cities: From the Right to the City to the Urban Revolution*, London: Verso.

Harvey, D. (2000) *Spaces of Hope*, Berkeley, Los Angeles: University of California Press.

Hays, K. M. (2010) *Architecture's Desire, Reading the Late Avant-Garde*, Cambridge, MA: MIT Press.

Hays, K. M., Ed. (2000) *Architecture Theory Since 1968*, Cambridge, MA: Columbia Books On Architecture/MIT Press.

Hays, K. M., Ed. (1998) *Oppositions Reader*, New York: Princeton Architectural Press.

Heynen, H. (1999) *Architecture and Modernity: A Critique*, Cambridge, MA: MIT Press.

Lefebvre, H. (2014) Toward and Architecture of Enjoyment, Stanek, Ł., ed., trans. Robert Bonono, Minneapolis: University of Minnesota Press.

Lefebvre, H. (1992/2004) 'Elements of Rhythmanalysis: An Introduction to Understanding Rhythms', in *Rhythmanalysis: Space, Time and Everyday Life*, trans. Stuart Elden and Gerald Moore, New York & London: Continuum, pp. 1–69.

Lefebvre, H. (1992/2004) *Rhythmanalysis: Space, Time and Everyday Life*, trans. Stuart Elden and Gerald Moore, New York & London: Continuum.

Lefebvre, H. (1987) 'The Everyday and Everydayness', trans. Christine Levich, *Yale French Studies*, no. 73, Everyday Life, pp. 7–11.

Lefebvre, H. (1986/2009) 'International Competition for the New Belgrade Urban Structure Improvement, in *Autogestion, or Henri Lefebvre in New Belgrade*, eds. S. Bitter, H. Weber and J. Derksen, Berlin: B Sternberg Press and Fillip Editions, pp. 1–32.

Lefebvre, H. (1986) 'Hors du Centre, point de Salut?' (No Salvation Away From the Centre?), *Espaces Temps*, 33, pp. 17–19, reprinted in *Writings on Cities* (1996), trans. Eleanore Kofman and Elizabeth Lebas, Oxford: Wiley-Blackwell, pp. 205–208.

Lefebvre, H. (1978) 'Space and the State', *De l'État, vol. 4*, Union Générale d'Éditions, Paris, reprinted in Brenner, N. and Elden, S., eds. (2009) *State, Space, World: Selected Essays*, trans. Gerald Moore, Neil Brenner and Stuart Elden, Minneapolis: University of Minnesota Press, pp. 224–253.

Lefebvre, H. (1976) 'Réflexions sur la politique de l'espace' (Reflections on the Politics of Space), *Espaces et sociétés* 1, pp. 3–12, reprinted in *Antipode* 8, no. 2, pp. 30–37, trans. Michael J. Enders, reprinted in Brenner, N. and Elden, S., eds. (2009) *State, Space, World: Selected Essays*, trans. Gerald Moore, Neil Brenner and Stuart Elden, Minneapolis: University of Minnesota Press.

Lefebvre, H. (1974/1991) *The Production of Space*, trans. Donald Nicholson-Smith, Oxford: Wiley-Blackwell.

Lefebvre, H. (1972) 'Preface', in Boudon, P. *Lived-in Architecture: Le Corbusier's Pessac Revisited*, trans. Gerald Onn, Cambridge, MA: MIT Press.

Lefebvre, H. (1971/1984) *Everyday Life in the Modern World*, trans. Sacha Rabinovitch, New Brunswick, NJ: Transaction Publishers.

Lefebvre, H. (1970) 'Reflections on the Politics of Space', reprinted in Brenner, N. and Elden, S., eds. (2009) *State, Space, World: Selected Essays*, trans. Gerald Moore, Neil Brenner and Stuart Elden, Minneapolis: University of Minnesota Press, pp. 167–184.

Lefebvre, H. (1970) 'Time and History', from *La Fin de l'histoire*, Paris: Éditions de Minuit, and 2ᵉ édn. (2001), Paris: Anthropos, reprinted in Lefebvre, H. (2003) *Key Writings*, eds. S. Elden, E. Lebas and E. Kofman (trans. unspecified), New York: Continuum, pp. 177–187.

Lefebvre, H. (1968a) *The Right to the City*, reprinted in *Writings on Cities* (1996), trans. E. Kofman and E. Lebas, Oxford: Wiley-Blackwell, pp. 63–181.

Lefebvre, H. (1968b) *The Sociology of Marx*, trans. Norbert Guterman, London: Allen Lane, The Penguin Press.

Lefebvre, H. (1966) 'Preface to the Study of the Habitat of the "Pavillon" ', from Raymond, H., Raymond, M-G., Haumont, Norbert and Coornaert, M., *L'Habitat pavillonnaire*, Paris: Éditions du CRU, reprinted as 'Introduction à l'étude de l'habitat paillonnaire' (2001) in *Du Rural à l'urbain, 3ᵉ édn*, Paris: Anthropos, reprinted in Lefebvre, H. (2003) *Key Writings*, eds. S. Elden, E. Lebas and E. Kofman (trans. unspecified), New York: Continuum, pp. 121–135.

Lefebvre, H. (1962/1995) *Introduction to Modernity: Twelve Preludes, September 1959–May 1961*, trans. John Moore, London: Verso.

Lefebvre, H. (1961a/2008) *Critique of Everyday Life Volume II, Foundations for a Sociology of the Everyday*, trans. John Moore, London: Verso.

Lefebvre, H. (1961b/2003) 'Elucidations', from *Critique de la vie Quotidienne II: Fondements d'une sociologie de la quotidinneté*, Paris: L'Arche, pp. 7–8, reprinted in Lefebvre, H. *Key Writings*, eds. S. Elden, E. Lebas and E. Kofman, (trans. unspecified), New York: Continuum, pp. 84–87.

Lefebvre, H. (1947/1958/2008) *Critique of Everyday Life Volume 1*, trans. John Moore, London: Verso.

Lefebvre, H. and Régulier, C. (1986/2004) 'Essai de rythmanalyse des villes méditerranéennes', ('Attempt at the Rhythmanalysis of Mediterranean Cities'), *Peuples Méditerranéens*, 37, reprinted in Lefebvre, H. (1992) *Éléments de rythmanalyse: Introduction à la connaissance des rythmes*, Paris: Éditions Syllepse, pp. 97–109, and in English in *Rhythmanalysis: Space, Time and Everyday Life*, trans. Stuart Elden and Gerald Moore, New York & London: Continuum, pp. 87–100.

Lefebvre, H. and Régulier, C. (1985/2004) 'Le projet rythmanalytique' ('The Rhythmanalytical Project'), *Communications*, 41, pp. 191–199, reprinted in Lefebvre, H. (2004) *Rhythmanalysis: Space, Time and Everyday Life*, trans. Stuart Elden and Gerald Moore, New York & London: Continuum, pp. 71–83.

Levitas, R. (2013) *Utopia as Method: The Imaginary Reconstitution of Society*, Houndmills, Basingstoke, Hampshire: Palgrave Macmillan Ltd.

Levitas, R. (2000) 'For Utopia: The (limits of the) Utopian function in late capitalist society', *Critical Review of International Social and Political Philosophy*, vol. 3, no. 2, pp. 25–43.

Löwy, M. and Sayre R. (2001) *Romanticism Against the Tide of Modernity*, trans. Catherine Porter, Durham, NC: Duke University Press.

Marx, K. (September 1843) 'Letter to Arnold Ruge', quoted in Bloch, E. (1995) *The Principle of Hope* (*Das Prinzip Hoffnung*), Volume I, trans. Neville Plaice, Stephen Plaice and Paul Knight, Cambridge, MA: MIT Press, pp. 155–156.

Moylan, T. and Baccolini, R., Eds. (2007) *Utopia Method Vision, the Use Value of Social Dreaming*, Oxford: Peter Lang.

Ross, K. (1983/1997) 'Henri Lefebvre on the Situationists' (Lefebvre interviewed), trans. Kristin Ross, *October,* no. 79 (winter), pp. 69–83, available online at: www.notbored.org/lefebvre-interview.html [Accessed 30 August 2013].

Rowe, C. and Koetter, F. (1978) *Collage City*, Cambridge, MA: MIT Press.

Rykwert, J. (2002) *The Seduction of Place: The History and Future of Cities* [2000], New York: Vintage Books.

Rykwert, J. (1988) *The Idea of a Town: The Anthropology of Urban Form in Rome, Italy, and the Ancient World* [1963], Cambridge, MA: MIT Press.

Sarkis, H., Ed. (2001) *Le Corbusier's Venice Hospital*, Munich: Prestel.

Sargent, L. T. (2006) 'In Defense of Utopia', *Diogenes*, vol. 53, no. 1, pp. 11–17.

Shields, R. (1999) *Lefebvre, Love and Struggle, Spatial Dialectics*, Abingdon, Oxon: Routledge.

Somol, R. E., Ed. (1997) *Autonomy and Ideology, Positioning an Avant-Garde in America*, New York: Monacelli Press.

Stanek, L. (2011) *Henri Lefebvre on Space: Architecture, Urban Research, and the Production of Theory*, Minneapolis: University of Minnesota Press, 2011.

Strauven, F. (1998) *Aldo van Eyck: The Shape of Relativity*, trans. Victor J. Joseph, Amsterdam: Architectura & Natura Press.

Tafuri, M. (1973/1976) *Architecture and Utopia: Design and Capitalist Development*, trans. Barbara Luigia La Penta, Cambridge, MA: MIT Press.

van Eyck, A. (2008) *Aldo Van Eyck: Writings, vol. 1: The Child, the City and the Artist; vol. 2: Collected Articles and Other Writings 1947–1998*, The Netherlands: Sun Publishers.

van Eyck, A. (1999) *Aldo van Eyck, Works*, trans. Gregory Ball, Basel: Birkhauser.

van Eyck, A. (1967) 'Labyrinthian Clarity', *Forum*, July, p. 51, reprinted in *Aldo Van Eyck: Writings, vol. 1: The Child, the City and the Artist; vol. 2: Collected Articles and Other Writings 1947–1998*, The Netherlands: Sun Publishers, pp. 472–473.

van Eyck, A. (1962) 'Steps Toward a Configurative Discipline', *Forum* 3, August, pp. 81–93, reprinted in Ockman, J. (1993), *Architecture Culture: 1943–1968*, New York: Rizzoli and Columbia, pp. 348–360.

van Eyck, A. (1961) 'The Medicine of Reciprocity Tentatively Illustrated', *Forum*, April–May, reprinted in *Aldo Van Eyck: Writings, vol. 1: The Child, the City and the Artist; vol. 2: Collected Articles and Other Writings 1947–1998*, The Netherlands: Sun Publishers, pp. 312–323.

Vitruvius. (ca. first century BC/1914) *The Ten Books on Architecture*, trans. Morris Hicky Morgan, Cambridge, MA: Harvard University Press.

Index

Note: Page numbers in **bold** indicate photographs.

absolute 10; *a priori* character of 122; Cartesian notions of space as 113; conceptions of space 26; knowledge 48; love 48; as opposed to relative 120; problem 97; space 54, 55

absolutism 49; political 26

absolutist: abstractions 43; tendencies of Cartesian logic 59; tendency of Utopia 44

abstract(ing) 36, 42, 44, 46, 55, 63–4, 66, 96; abstract nature of mathematical theories 59; bureaucracies 73; in relation to Cartesian notions 113; as detached from quality 119; and mathematical detachment 59; opposite of 102; and reductive 90; representations of space as 62, 82; space 53–5, 66–7, 86, 92, 95, 120; space conceptualised as 80; space of capitalist production 55; systems 47; tendencies in architecture 65; and theoretical 81; thought 73; Utopia and its loss of edge 48; Utopia as abstract ideal 47; utopias 31; in relation to the visual 105

abstraction(s): as analogous to control 69; architecture imagined as 63; in relation to capitalist reduction and alienation 44; dissociative 44; dominance of 82; dominance of the visual in relation to 70; of dominant space 55; of mental space as separate from real space 59; in relation to power and reductionism 85; preventing the drift towards 78; in relation to the production of space 70; pure 96; representations of space as 8; of space 43, 59; space conceived of as 60, 79; of theoretical practices 592; Utopia characterized as 47

Adorno, Theodor W. 13

aesthetic(s) 116; apparent social and political neutrality of 110, 117; appreciation in relation to architecture 59; as bound to ethics 20; as delight alone 32–3; as divorced from ethics 65; Lefebvre's project in opposition to 32, 43

Alberti, Leon Battista, and Lefebvre 6

alienation: alternatives to (disalienation) 33–4, 104, 107;

in built environment 5, 52; in
relation to capitalism 24, 33, 44;
contribution of system-building
to 8; and dissolution of formal
boundaries 57; in relation to
division and isolation 57, 105; of
individuals 56; in relation to loss
of more directly experienced life
28; and modern city 23, 1059;
overcoming of 33; spread of 33
alternative(s): achievable step by
step 41; antithesis of 2; to
architectural practices 7, 11, 73,
85–6, 95, 103; arising out of the
everyday 49; being for 67; built
environment as testing ground
for 44; to capitalism, Marxism as
7; concrete 4; constant possibility
of 40; difficulty of imagining
9–11, 14, 18, 77, 118–19;
difficulty of realizing 32; ebbing
of hope for 34–5; foundation
of in the past (and in memory)
21, 25–6, 30, 31–2, 34, 41–2,
73–4; imagining 5, 6, 14, 22,
77, 91; persisting in memory 41,
42; realisation of 42; in relation
to Revolutionary Romanticism
33–4; self-determination as 32;
social and spatial arrangements
41; and social progress 29; to
space and life 36; to spatiality of
bureaucracy 40; suggested by
Lefebvre and van Eyck 7, 93–4;
as undefined 26; in relation to

Utopia 7, 18, 22, 34, 36, 38,
40–1, 46, 50–1, 66; utopianism
as a method for testing 45
Amsterdam Orphanage **8**, **94**
anticipatory: function of hope 30; in
opposition to compensatory 31
architect(s): and autonomy 35;
as brand 87; claims for their
work 49; counter-projects
86–7; as doctors of space
23; entrapment within the
dominant system 26–7;
fragmentation of the urban
environment 57, 77–8; and
industrial production 112–13;
Lefebvre's relevance for 1–17;
Lefebvrian 93–4, 103–4, 120–1,
129–30; practice habits of 34;
and rhythmanalyst 120–1;
separation of projects from
intended inhabitants 19, 56,
62–3, 73; settings for the
everyday 3; and the social 634;
as specialists 32, 61; threatened
with disappearance 117;
uncomfortable position of ix; and
Utopia 6, 40, 45–6, 51
architectural: education 24; form(s)
22, 65, 108; modernisms 31;
practice 2, 7, 34, 92, 95; theory
6, 130; urbanism 35
architecture: and modernity 19;
contemporary 8, 24; high
modern 76–7; modern 12, 19,
39, 49, 112; modern movement

in 89; orthodox modern 5, 35, 37–8, 100; postmodernist 13, 22

Aristotle 59

Augé, Marc 35

authoritarianism: as analogous to absolutism 26; closed 26; Lefebvre's aversion to 26; masculine principle as a form of 84; spatial closure as a form of 26–7; of spatial closure counterbalanced by open-endedness of social processes 123; *see also* absolutism

autonomy project in architecture 35, 37, 76–7

Baudrillard, Jean 7

beauty: ebbing of in the modern world 32–3; as a kind of comprehensiveness 32–3; made up of eurhythmically interrelated parts 32

Benjamin, Walter 13

Bentham, Jeremy 9; *see also* panopticon

Bloch, Ernst: capture of architecture by late capitalism 25, 103; conception of Concrete Utopia 30–1; in relation to Frankfurt School 13; fruitless *Empty-Possible* of *Abstract-Utopias* 31; on hollow space of capitalism 5; philosopher of hope 10; similarity of concept of *Real-Possible* to

Lefebvre's concept of *Possible-Impossible* 31

blueprint(s): as totalising or absolutist 18, 31, 89

body: absence of from architectural imaginings 97; answer to limits of architecture and urbanism reside in 98; architects who recollect the rhythms of in their work 103; in relation to building 99, 109, 113, 116; capitalism's contempt for 117; disciplined to the demands of bureaucratisation 118; importance of to Lefebvre's work 125; imposition of metric organisation on 113; as neglected in philosophy 103; as primary referent in built environment 103, 109, 116; reclaiming a place for 104; recuperation of centrality of to architecture 121; rhythmanalyst listen to and learns rhythms from 102; scale of 109, 113, 116; as a rhythmic instrument 105; scale of in dialogue with scale of the world 127

built environment: alienating conditions of 32; blighting of 18; as characterised by non-places (spaces that are strange, homogeneous, rationalized, constraining and dislocated) 35, 57; countering the concretisation of alienation in with Utopia 52; disillusion and emptiness in as product of alienation 56; as indifferent to the facts of the body 97; influence of neoliberalism on 39; inscription of alienation in 5; Lefebvre's preoccupation with as primarily social 32; made more sophisticated by applying and methods of rhythmanalysis 103; rhythmanalysis as method for countering alienation in 104; shaped by global capitalist spatial practices 34; as stage upon which life is played out 44; van Eyck and potential for it to be more humane 100

bureaucratic: abstracting tendencies of 73; disciplining of the body 118; organisation 64; organization of towns 32; 105–6; resistance of everyday to 101; society 36; spatiality 26; suppression of quotidian 33; surveillance 49; tendency toward bloat 40; Utopia as an alternative to 40

Calatrava, Santiago 87

capitalism: and abstract space 66; and alienation 23, 33, 57; alternatives to 7, 29, 42; before capitalism 33–4; capture of architecture by 5, 9, 14, 16, 25, 92, 117; destructive capacities of 117, 125; and division(s) 28,40, 64, 77; and fragmentation 60, 77;

global 7, 12, 14, 18, 34, 66, 68; hegemonic space of 60; limiting perspectives of 22, 27, 38, 119; Marx's critique of 12, 40; pre-capitalist as critique of 21–2, 27, 30, 33, 41–2, 117; and the production of space 11; and rationality 18; and reductionism 13; and reproduction 68; as ruthlessly pragmatic 40; spatialization of 55, 60–1, 63, 75; state 11; vocation for constant change 24

capitalist: consumption 35; production 21, 23, 37, 55, 63–4; realism 7, 27, 35, 37, 103; space 22; transition from pre-capitalist production 21–2

Cartesian, cartesianism: in relation to abstraction and abstract space 26, 59, 92, 103, 113

centrality: refusal of in Mediterranean cities 114–15

centralized power 60

Centre Georges Pompidou (Pompidou Centre) 108–9, 110, 112

CIAM (Congrès International d'Architecture Moderne) 19

citizen(s) 115

city (cities): capitalist 25, 42, 105; contemporary 8, 24, 31–2, 57, 114; Mediterranean 108, 112–15; modern 12, 23, 39–40, 64, 109, 114–15; neocapitalist;

140   INDEX

neoliberal 11, 34, 39, 63, 104; planning 37–8; pre-capitalist 41–2; pre-modern 74

code(s) 82; collapse of earlier 72–3; in relation to consensus 75; in relation to contents of social and spatial in relation to ideology 76–7; in relation to contents of social and spatial practices 72–3; dialectical character of 72; earliest spatial 78; language 73; of linear perspective 76; a new spatial 74, 77–8; and relations of production 82; in relation to social and intimate relations 114; spatial 72–4, 77, 79, 83; as a system of space 72; unitary 79

common language 75

community 1; building 126; effect of capitalist production on 21–2, 28, 33; social processes of 8–9

community life 22, 33

compensatory 31

concrete: alternatives 4; analyses 46; arriving at by way of the abstract 96; arriving at by way of the body 105; arriving at through experience 102; beach 108; conditions 46, 78; considerations 73; constraints 67; as definite 44; experience 82; form 26–7, 43; idea of history 48; Lefebvre's focus on 81; mixers 69; practice as 78–9; practices 8–9; presence 74; proposals 55–6; solutions 26; space as 79; steps 31; synthesis 32; times 120; universal 53; Utopia 30, 44, 48

conditions: concrete 46, 78; existing 5–6, 25, 40; spatial 22, 33, 77

consciousness 1, 10, 25–7, 30–1, 35, 37, 41, 43–4, 57, 68, 74, 91, 96–7, 104–6, 116

consensus 75; banal 59; ideology as an adjunct of 77; neoliberal 2, 91

Constant (Constant Nieuwenhuys) 7, 93

consumed 114

consumerism 36

consumer(s) 18, 28

consumption 23, 70, 105; of architecture 57; capitalist 35; destinations of and for 107; domain of 112; organized 9; programmed 64; public space as a stage of 114; spaces of 11

counterexample 69

counter-plan(s) 56, 86

counter-practices 7, 38, 93

counter-project(s) 56, 59, 85–7

counterproposal, counter-proposals 14, 35, 85–6

counter-spaces 74, 85, 95–6

depoliticising Lefebvre: 91–2

Descartes, René 59

desire(s) 14, 18, 26, 28, 41, 66, 103, 116, 119, 129

development: capitalist 12; central control of 112; economic 24; fashions 116; project(s) 111; real estate investment and 25, 37, 107; uneven geographical 123; urban 107

dialectical: analysis 43, 100 (triadic character of in relation to Hegel and Marx); character of codes 72; reason 46; relationship between possible and impossible 43, 48, 68; Utopia, 123; utopianism 34, 42–4, 123; van Eyck's approach as 100

difference(s): and Mediterranean cities 114–15; architects' stake in ix; coexistence of 78; eradication of 61, 92, 96; excluded and generated by repetition 97; moments of 105; persistence of 96; spaces of 113

dressage 118

empty-possible 31

Engels, Friedrich 89

ethics: as divorced from aesthetics 65; in relation to aesthetics 20

everyday: analysis of 62, 122; banality of 36; in collusion with abstract and impersonal forces 36; colonisation of by clockwork time and capital 119; complex character of 36; concrete conditions of 46; deformed by positivism 33; discourse 74; disruption of 94; dissolution of 33; dominated by spectacle 35; as the heart of the possible 48; metric organisation of 113; object of rhythmanalyst's study 105; pseudo-fête as disconnected from 112; realm 78; and resistance 14; reunified 33; rhythms observable in 101; settings for the flourishing of 34; shot through and traversed by great cosmic rhythms 119; as site of alternatives 4, 6, 10, 36, 49, 51, 105–6; as site of resistance and conformity 36, 48, 101, 118–19; tacit utopianism of 107; transforming 37; unitary theory of 33; utopian moment of 107; where past and present intersect 14

everyday life: in relation to architecture and cities 124; as convivial 34; critique(s) of 8, 10–11, 14, 33, 43–4; deprivation of 27; destructive effect of progress on 28; dialectical utopianism as a method for critiquing 43–4; directly lived 41–2; dissolution of 33; domination by apparently totalising forces 9, 67, 77; equivalent of programmed consumption and location of bureaucratic organisation 64;

142   INDEX

full and active participation in 32; gap between architect's and planners products and 56–7; main theme of Lefebvre's thinking 2, 54; in New York City **15**; not a generic good 64; recuperation of 39; renewed forms of 26–7; rhythmanalysis of 95, 105; site of resistance to bureaucratic organisation, divisions of capitalist production and requirements of the state 64; social and intimate rhythms of 127; source of resistance to abstract space of capitalist production 55, 64; space, time and 13; and its spaces 33; splendor of 27; transformation of 89; van Eyck's architecture as counterforms to 93

exchange value 63, 70, 72, 103 107

experience(s): aesthetics divorced from 65; collective action informed by 4; concrete 82; directly lived 28, 47, 87, 96; and identity 3; individual 3; of individuals and groups 63; lived 58–9, 63; passive 83; and rhythmanalyst 102; as sources of alternatives 21; theory of rhythms founded on 91

Florence, Italy: *centro storico* 29; as counter-example 69; as Lefebvre's favourite city 28

Foster, Norman 87, 88

Fourier, François Marie Charles 89

Frankfurt School 13

functionalism: technical 65; reductive 103

future(s): built upon present reform efforts 21, 28, 34, 43–4; built upon the past 125; hopes for 18; limitations to thinking of in terms of progress and revolution 34; as *not-yet* 34; as part of dialectic triad (including also past and present) 100; possible 14, 33; tension between past and 33–4; Utopia as a project of 18–19, 66; Utopia as anticipation of 41

Giedion, Sigfried 19,120

global capitalism: as dominant system 7, 14; in relation to extreme rationality and quantification 18; and extreme separation 68; impossibility of architecture under the conditions of 12, 14; in relation to technological Utopia 66; *see also* capitalism

golden age 21

harmony 32, 64, 67, 96, 99

Harvey, David 12, 26

hegemony: definition of 60; Lefebvre's target 61–2; refused in the Mediterranean 114

Hertzberger, Herman 6

homogeneity 57; refused in the Mediterranean 114; spatial 72

hope(s): as abstract 44; anticipatory function of 30; Bloch as philosopher of 10, 25; ebbing of 34–5; extinguishing of 18; false 19; for the future 18; as opposite of despair 41

horizons of possibility: expansion of 34; limitation of 18

human body: centrality of to architecture's social vision 121; as primary reference in the built environment 103; scale of 109; as subject, object and model for social structuring and restructuring, and architecture and cities 121

idealism 30, 37

ideology: dominant 61; embedded in gesture 66; in relation to hegemony 60; identification of with a particular space 82; and knowledge 41; material as carrier of 61; as necessary adjunct of consensus 77; of originality 87; requires a space 76; sporting 117

interdisciplinarity, interdisciplinary 64, 101–2

intimate, intimately: knowledge 110; and social relations 114; rhythms 127; separation from the state-political 122

Jameson, Fredric: and the crisis of architecture 5; Lefebvre's influence on 13; as theorist of total closure 10, 103

labour: and active body 95; division of 28, 40, 57, 60, 64; preindustrial 112

Le Corbusier: blamed for failures of modern architecture 19; city plans as abstract and Cartesian 92; Lefebvre's ambivalence towards 92–3; *promenade architecturale* 121; unbuilt Venice Hospital project 93

Levitas, Ruth 18

Libeskind, Daniel 87

limits of the given 31

lived, conceived and perceived 68, 75, 82, 84

mall space: as dominant architectural form and function 108

marketization 18

Marx, Karl: and architectural theory 12–13; and Bloch's concrete utopia 30–1; and dialectical analysis 100; centrality of to Lefebvre's thinking 2; critique of capitalism 12, 40; as a great Utopian 89; limitations of ideas for Lefebvre 12, 34, 40–1; political theories of 7; pronounced dead ix; and uncompleted work of the past 3; and Utopia 13, 39; value of for thinking through problems of architecture 12

Marxism, Marxist: alternative to capitalism 7; applied 40; critique of architecture 92; Lefebvre's commitment to 38–9; Lefebvre's expansion of 8, 12, 21, 41, 91; resurgence of ix; spatial limitations of 7; understanding Lefebvre in the context of 92

master narratives 22

May 1968 34

Mediterranean Cities 108, 112–15

modernism: architectural and urban 19, 22, 31, 111; overcoming 22

modernity (Modernity): architecture and 19; architecture of identified with Le Corbusier and CIAM 19; confrontation with by Romanticism and Utopia 1; crisis of 31–2; critique of 21–2; critique of from pre-modern position 21, 35; decline of 22; and destruction of generally legible spatial codes 73; destructive forces of 33; dissociation of time from space in 54; and everydayness 36; Lefebvre's engagement with problems of 12; myths of 34; overconfidence of 22; progress of 28; promise of recollected

by Romanticism 19; proximity between and archaism 110; solvent aspects of 29; in tension with social justice 1; threshold of 53; tradition and 28; transformations in the name of 116; unhinged from past 27

More, Sir Thomas 48

Morris, William: and architecture 19; correspondence of Lefebvre's thinking with 20–1; as social reformer 5

Municipal Baths, Vals, Switzerland 103; **121**

neocapitalist, neocaptialism: as dominant ideology 61; space 60, 68; system 23

neoliberal, neoliberalism: city 34; consensus 2, 91; emphasis on vacuity 63; influence on social life and built environment 39; production of space 104; spaces 11, 91; spatial practices 34

Newcastle upon Tyne: computer image **58**; Waterloo Square **50**

New York City: everyday life in **15**; Sixth Avenue **71**; World Trade Center 117

nineteenth century 5, 19–20, 33, 42, 64, 75, 79, 114

non-places 35

Not Yet (Not-Yet) 21, 25, 34, 43, 45

optimism 30, 86, 116, 125

other possibilities

Panopticon (panoptic) 9; 49

Paris: bears imprint of what it hides
111; *Centre Georges Pompidou*
108 **110**; loss of traditional
characteristics 111; May 1968
34; and the Mediterranean 108;
project for in 2000 46; shopping
mall in 117

past (the): achievements of 21;
cities 26; content of Utopia 19;
as critique of the present 74;
extoling of as morbidly nostalgic
111; as generative 34; idealised
33; images of 22; impossibility
of return to 31; intersection
with present 14, 21; Lefebvre's
engagement with 20, 28, 32,
114, 125; modernity unhinged
from 27; as part of present-future
triad 100; practices 15; pre-
capitalist 33; as radical 29; source
of alternatives 14, 29–31, 34, 73;
tensions between and future 33;
towns as source for future ones
32; uncompleted work of 30–1

Piano, Renzo 108, **110**

place and occasion 120–1

planner(s): and abstraction 82; claims
for their work 49; and counter-
projects 86–7; as doctors of
space 23; entrapment within

the dominant system 26–7;
and fragmentation of the urban
environment 77–8; practice
habits of 34; separation of plans
from intended beneficiaries
56, 62–3; and settings for the
everyday 34; as specialists 32;
and Utopia 40, 45–7, 51

planning 35, 46, 97; city 37–8;
modern 49; and omission of
space and place 105; social 66;
urban 5, 25, 35, 49, 65–6, 73;
and urban design 1–2

poetic 102, 123

political power 53, 67, 74, 86, 107

polyrhythmia, polyrhythmic,
polyrhythmically 91, 114, 120

positivism: certainty of control as
the absence of thought 40,
42; colonisation of everyday
by 33; insidious presence of
in French Marxism 21; and
modern architecture 19; system
of defined 19; Utopia which
masquerade as 46, 49; Utopias
as method to overcome 39

possibility, possibilities: of alternative
spaces 77; certainties of control
mask 118; endlessly open 26;
everyday as the locus of 105;
horizons of 34; Lefebvre as a
partisan of 51; Lefebvre's project
of 51; limits of 25; modern
as locus of 31; turned in on

themselves 26; utopian vision of 39, 42, 43–4

possible–impossible 14, 21, 31, 34, 42–3, 47–8, 95, 105, 107

postmodernism (postmodern): 7, 13, 22, 92

potential futures 18

power: centralized 60; Lefebvre's disputations with 61–2; political 53, 67, 74, 86, 107; relations 61–2; spatialization of 116; system-building as an expression of 85; vast resources of 86

pragmatic, pragmatism 3–4; 26; 40

pre-capitalist: architecture 117; city 41–2; modes of life 27; organization of production 21–2; past 33; social arrangements 30

pre-industrial: city 25; organisation of production 21

pre-modern: city superior to modern city 74; as critique of modernity 21, 33–4; Lefebvre's reference to the social and spatial forms of 21, 25, 33–4, 112; space 82; towns embody something missing from modern ones 31, 33–4; Venice, Italy 115

producers and consumers: separations between 28

product(s): buildings as 57; dominance of visual in 70; in relation to an ideology of originality 87; reproducibility and standardization of 54, 87; status of space as 70; vanquish works 69; as opposed to works 63, 70, 72

production: architectural 37; capitalist 21, 23, 37, 55, 63–4; conditions of 20; industrial 64, 113; prevailing modes of 60, 63; relations of 37, 62, 80, 82; representations of the relations of production 62; of social space 59, 62; of space 1–2, 6, 8, 11, 13, 26, 53–60, 62, 64, 66, 70, 82–3, 85, 88–9, 92, 95, 104, 129

Production of Space, The 53–90

progress: faith in 21; industrial 21; modernity 21, 34; social 29; technological 28–9

project of a different society 55

psychology 102, 123

public space 62, 107–9, 114–15

qualitative 3, 49, 70, 84, 96, 112–13

quantitative 49, 84, 96, 112, 119

radical critique 23, 53, 114

real possibility 24, 42

real-possible 31

reductionism 5, 13, 37, 85, 101

reform: architectural 3; artistic 20; political 3; social 5, 23, 25; spatial 23, 25

regeneration 37, 110

relativism 22

relativity: of rhythms 104, 120, 123; van Eyck's conception of 6, 121

Renaissance 6; representations of space 75–6; shattering of space inherited from 74–5; spatial practices of 72–4; town 76, 79; Tuscany 26, 28, 75

repetition ix, 5, 69–70, 99, 118; cyclical 96–7

representation(s) 2, 58, 76; architectural 82; cosmological 84; decorative 109; as distancing 104; dominant 56, 82; habits of 11; partial 65; problems of 58; of reality 47; of the relations of production 62; of society 62; of space 54; 62, 75–6, 79, 81–2, 84, 115; visual 58

representational space(s) 62, 76, 79, 81, 83–4

restrictive realism 30

reworking what exists 23

rhythm(s): analysis of 102, 106; of bodies and social activities 96–7; cyclical 97, 113; of daily life 80; and difference 96; as inflection of space in time 120; interdependence of spatial and temporal in 120; internalised through repetition 118–19; Lefebvre's concept of 98–9, 102; as non-mechanical 119; not movement 96; as rational

and least rational 96–8; relativity of 120, 122; of steps 115–16; urban 115; van Eyck's preoccupation with 121

rhythmanalysis 13; as alternative to Cartesianism 103; asserts importance of spatial considerations in understanding of social life 122; body as central to 91, 95–6; as defence against totalising thought 96; and the everyday 101, 105; method of 106; as new science and field of knowledge 95–6; present as the object of 105; relevance for architectural practice 94–5, 97, 105, 107, 121; returns body to consciousness 97; reveals moments of change and transformation 104–5, 119; reveals relation between space and time 122; starts with abstract to arrive at concrete 96; and van Eyck 99, 121; and Zumthor 121

Rhythmanalysis: Space, Time and Everyday Life 13, 91–127, 129

Rice, Peter 108

rites 114

Rogers, Richard 108, **110**

Romanticism, romanticism: agonistic 26, 28; and classicism 43; concentration on loss and renewal 28; Lefebvre's 31; new

18, 21; nineteenth-century 33;
old 21; radical 34; revolutionary
21, 33; and Utopia 1–2, 11–12,
21–2, 30, 34, 49; as a utopian
anticipation 30

Rome, Italy: 69, **75**, **84**; Ancient 81–4

Rowe, Colin 86

rural: communities 27; decline of a
way of life in 28; deprivation of
everyday life in 27; ground 81;
pre-capitalist conditions of 22;
sociology 21; unity with urban 79

Ruskin, John: and architecture 5;
correspondences of Lefebvre's
thinking to 20–1; utopia socialist
reform vision of 19

Sage Gateshead **88**

science 102; dominance of 97;
fiction 66; as insufficient 98;
rhythmanalysis as 95; of space
59, 64–5; and technology 97,
103; and Utopia 68

self-determination 32

shopping mall(s): dominance of 35;
as key setting of daily life 35–6;
in the Marais 108, 117; ubiquity
of 69

Siena, Italy 69

Situationists: Constant's association
with 93; Lefebvre's association
with 7, 93

social: activities 10, 97, 113;
conditions 25; 64; critique 22;

dimension 6, 73, 76; dreaming
77; emptiness 5; engagement
2; engineering 67; housing 25;
imaginary 18; imagination 7;
justice 1; life 11, 13, 21–2, 27,
34, 39–42, 51–2, 59–60, 63,
65, 67–8, 73–4, 79, 83, 92, 98,
101, 113, 117, 122; planning
66; practice(s) 55, 59, 61, 72,
74, 76, 81–2; process(es) 2, 8–9,
64, 123; realm 59, 63; reform
23, 25; relations 12, 81 87, 98,
101, 125; richness 117; rituals
10; sciences 105; settings 22;
space(s) 3, 11, 54, 59, 61–2, 65,
72, 76, 80–1, 95

social and intimate rhythms 114, 127

sociology 41, 102, 123; inspired by
Marx 41; rural 21

space(s): absolute 54; abstract
53–5, 66–7, 86, 95; capitalist
22, 105; of the city 62, 74; as
commodity **58**, 63, 68–9, 70,
103, 117; conceived 75, 82, 84;
conceptualized 82; contradictory
54; criticism of 23, 56; directly
lived 62–3, 83–4; dominated
83; empty 53; Euclidean 73;
geometrical 59; hegemonic
60–1; historical 54; lived 82;
mental 59–60; non-hegemonic
60–1; as product 70, 103;
production of 1–2, 6, 8, 11,
13, 26, 53–60, 62, 64, 66, 70,

82–3, 85, 88–9, 92, 95, 104, 129; public 114–15; real 1, 59; relative 54; of representation 54; representational 62, 76, 79, 81, 83–4; representations of 54, 62, 76, 79, 81–2, 84; represented 82; science of 59, 64–5; social 54, 59, 61–2, 65, 72, 76, 80–1, 95; of social practice 61; system of 72; and time, 118, 120, 122; unitary theory of system of space 61; urban 61–2, 91, 113

Spaces of Hope 12,123, 130

spatial: alternatives 50–1; arrangements 22, 41, 73; closure 26, 123; codes 72–4; conditions 22, 33, 73; context 122; form(s) 26, 30, 123; homogeneity 72; practice(s) 64, 67–9, 72–81, 84–5, 93; praxis 54; reality 23; reform 23, 25; relations 22–3; richness 13

specialization 39–40, 44–6, 64

spectacle 35, 37, 39, 105, 107, 111–12

state(s) 2, 9, 30, 64, 53, 57, 79, 83, 92, 107, 113, 115, 117; apparatuses 117; capitalism 11; consciousness 36–7; controls 55; domination 91; interests 105–6; -political (order) 110–11, 122; socialism 39

substructure 23, 36–7

suburbs 23, 57, 64

subversive 61, 99

supermodernity 35

superstructure 23, 37

system(s) 25, 64, 89, 119; abstract 47; alternative to capitalism 7; antithesis of 53, 85, 89; of architectural representation 46–7; base twelve 112; building 53, 85, 89; capitalist 23; closed 39, 118; coded 73; coherent 83; of control 60; critique of 22–3; decimal 113; dominant 9–11, 14–15, 25–7, 60, 91; duodecimal 112; economic 7; existing 36; making 90; metric 113; neocapitalist 23; of organisation 22; philosophical 19; political 14; prevailing 77; of production 60; of space 72; total 103; totalising 35; underlying 24–5; universalizing 35; world 10

systematization(s) 61–2, 90

Tafuri, Manfredo: and the crisis of architecture 14; 16, 34, 86, 103; different conclusions from Lefebvre 7; influence of 12; and the limits of architecture 5, 86, 103; as Marxist historian 7; as theorist of total closure 10, 14, 34

technique 114

temporal: and spatial 120, 123; reach 22; richness 13

theory: architecture 2, 6, 7, 13, 15–16, 33, 37, 97, 124, 129; beyond system-building 53; critical 66–7, 74; deprivation of 100–1; of the everyday 33; explosion 16, 37; Le Corbusier's 92–3; of moments 94–5; operative 85; practice and 2, 4, 33, 77; for practice 8–9; as a product of Utopia 38, 40; of rhythms 91,102; separation from practice 40, 60, 97, 100–1; of space 61; and transduction 44–5

Thermal Baths Vals 103

time: clockwork 119; everyday 122; free 122; historical 122; lived 122; measured 122; work 122

time and space (space and time) 118, 120, 122

topography of Mediterranean cities 114–15

totalising: practices 91; systems 35; thought 96; urban projects 25; Utopia 43, 89

totalitarianism 26 *see also* absolutism

totality 10, 14, 120, 124

towns 28, 32, 86,91; contemporary 31–2; earlier 31; layout of 114; lunar 113; medieval 79; Mediterranean 114; modern 32, 69; new 31, 44; Nordic 113; pre-modern 31; self-determination in making 32; solar 113; ugly and boring 32–3; Western 75

tradition 15, 28, 125; Greek 74; Romantic 21; Western 71

transduction 95; defined 44–5; method for reforming Utopia 44; relevance for architecture 47, 49; reveals experimental propensity of Utopia 46

Tuscany 26, 28

twentieth century 5, 12, 19, 73, 93

twenty-first century 5

tyranny 26 *see also* absolutism

unequal societies 18, 40

unthinkable: alternatives 5; fundamentally utopian 38

urban: design 1–2; designer(s) 34, 39, 51, 61, 63; development 107; environment 57, 77, 105; forms 112; innovations 25; milieu 42; modernism 19; planners 40, 49; planning 5, 25, 65; practices 11, 34, 37, 103, 114; projects 123; realm 78; redevelopment 49; renewal 25; research 49; settings 97, 99, 101; space 61–2; 91, 113–14; surgery 24

urbanism 5, 8, 10, 19, 37, 63, 81, 98,100, 103; architectural 35; Le Corbusier's 92–3; Lefebvre's model of 114; social dimension of 76; split between architecture and 69; and technological utopia 66–7; van Eyck's 93

urbanists 23, 73, 78, 82, 93

use value 63, 70

Utopia(s): abstract 31, 47–8; and anticipation 41; applied 41; and architecture 37, 47; concrete 30, 48; constitutive 43; critical 66; degenerate 25; dialectical 46, 48, 67–8, 123; easy 90; experimental 45–6; as furthest edge of the possible 89; as good non place 48; as good place 48; of impossibility 89; Lefebvre and 34; as method 18, 20, 43; negative 67; as no place 48; no thought without 48; pathological 43; positive 51–2; positivism masquerading as 49; as possible-impossible 48, 67–8; practical side of 50; prognosticating 47; propensity for research 50; of real projects 89; as recuperated social life 51; rejection of 88; and Romanticism 1, 19, 22, 30, 49; of social process 123; of spatial closure 123; technological 66–7; theoretical 44; as theory of the distantly possible 48; totalising 89; urgent 51–2

utopian: alternative 18; anticipation 30; architecture 19, 49; Christian 19; dimension of *The Production of Space* 66; envisioning 18; experiments 41; Lefebvre as 51–2; Lefebvre's counter-projects as 87–8; Lefebvre's thinking as 51; Lefebvre's writing as 38; longing 18; Marxism 39; method 44; moment of the everyday 107; positive 19; practice 38, 41; project 55; promise 19–20; prospect of Lefebvre 51; register of Romanticism 21; removal of 13; Renaissance town as 79; revolutionary 42; and romantic 21–2, 41–2; Socialist(s) 19, 42; and transduction 44–5; as unhealthy 22; vision 39, 43

utopianism(s): anti- 6, 39; anticipation 30; concrete 44; constitutive 43; critique 37; dialectical 42–4, 123; experimental 20, 34, 45; Lefebvre's 7–8, 35–6, 36; method 30; moment 36; near inescapability of 39; negative 67; pathological; 43, 46; practice 34; renewed 37; and Romanticism 2; spatiotemporal 123; tacit 107; techno- 108; technological 67; traditional 26; and transduction 45

Vals (Thermal Baths at) 103, **121**

van Eyck, Aldo: Amsterdam Orphanage **8**, **94**; anthropological approach to architecture 6; architecture of as counterform to Lefebvre's thinking 7; collaboration with Constant 7, 93; Constant as link to Lefebvre 7, 93; as contentious figure in architecture 93; correspondences with Lefebvre's work 98–101, 103, 120–1; importance of social dimension and everyday to theory and practice of 6; influence on Le Corbusier 93; as Lefebvrian architect 6, 93–4, 129; radical implications of his work 7, 93

Venice, Italy 83, 115
Vitruvius (Marcus Vitruvius Pollio) 32, 79

Zumthor, Peter: childlike wonder and bodily events as source of designs 103; as exception 103; Municipal Baths, Vals, Switzerland 103, **121**; work in relation to rhythm and rhythmanalysis 121